GOOD BOUNDARIES AND GOODBYES

LOVING OTHERS WITHOUT LOSING THE BEST OF WHO YOU ARE

STUDY GUIDE + STREAMING VIDEO

SIX SESSIONS

LYSA TERKEURST

#1 *New York Times* Bestselling Author

Good Boundaries and Goodbyes Study Guide

Requests for information should be addressed to:

HarperChristian Resources, 3900 Sparks Dr. SE, Grand Rapids, Michigan 49546

ISBN 978-0-310-14035-1 (softcover)

ISBN 978-0-310-14036-8 (ebook)

HarperChristian Resources titles may be purchased in bulk for church, business, fundraising, or ministry use. For information, please e-mail ResourceSpecialist@ChurchSource.com.

First Printing November 2022 / Printed in the United States of America

Contents

Letter from Lysa

Hello, Friend!

As we begin this journey together, learning about good boundaries and goodbyes, I want you to know that I recognize none of this is easy. But it is good. Good for our relationships. And good for our own personal health. You see, when we have good boundaries, we're better able to fulfill the two greatest commandments in the Bible: to love God and love others.

That's our whole aim with this study guide, to grow in our capacity to love more fully and more deeply.

Because some of the topics we'll be discussing within these pages are so very tender, I truly wish we could sit across a table and open our Bibles together. I understand the devastating heartbreak that happens when good boundaries have been broken. So, it is with utmost prayer that I offer you this study.

We're going to see that boundaries have been God's idea all along. He designed us and therefore, He knows what we need to thrive as we pursue healthy relational dynamics. God's design is for us to live in community with others without losing the best of who we are. Love is what should draw us together, not tear us apart.

What you hold in your hands is the culmination of years' worth of my own study and the wise counsel from experts. Everything I have learned has been tried and tested through the crucible of real-life experiences and extensive theological study. In my own personal life, I have seen how better understanding biblical boundaries can transform some of the most challenging relationships and give me more confidence and reassurance that I'm walking in truth.

Knowing that God has already given us His truth and He's modeled boundaries since the very beginning of creation, helps us as we desire to make good relationships stronger and navigate unhealthy relationships with more clarity. We don't have to figure all of this out on our own. And we want to stay spiritually and emotionally healthy through it all.

This is my heart's desire for all of us… you, me, and those we want to love really well.

So, let's open up God's Word, and together let's marvel at what an intentionally good God we serve who has every answer for our deepest longings.

How to Use This Study Guide

GROUP SIZE

The *Good Boundaries and Goodbyes* video study is designed to be experienced in a group setting where meaningful discussions can take place. This could be a Bible study or a Sunday school class or any small group gathering. To facilitate greater participation, larger groups can split up into smaller circles of four to six people after the teaching video is viewed. If you do move into smaller groups, be sure to select one person in each group to act as the facilitator during the discussion time.

MATERIALS NEEDED

To gain the most from this study, each participant should have her own copy of this study guide, as well as her own copy of the book *Good Boundaries and Goodbyes*. This study guide contains notes from the video teachings, discussion questions, and personal study days that will deepen the learning between group sessions. Additionally, the leader will need to have the videos either on DVD or by digital stream/download. Streaming video access is included with the study guide.

WEEKLY SCHEDULE

At the beginning of each week, this study guide provides information on which chapters of the book should be read prior to the next group meeting. Each personal day of study will lead you deeper into the biblical content of the book. Please note: It is recommended that participants read the introduction and chapters 1–2 before the first group session. Below is a sample of the schedule you will find at the beginning of every new week.

BEFORE GROUP MEETING	Read Chapters ________ in *Good Boundaries and Goodbyes* book.
DURING GROUP MEETING	Watch teaching video for Session ________. Group discussion will follow on pages ________.
PERSONAL STUDY DAY 1	Pages ________.
PERSONAL STUDY DAY 2	Pages ________.
PERSONAL STUDY DAY 3	Pages ________.
PERSONAL STUDY DAYS 4 & 5	Read Chapters ________ in *Good Boundaries and Goodbyes* book. Complete any unfinished Personal Study activities.

TIMING

Time notations have been given for each heading of the group meeting sections of the study. These indicate the *actual* time of the video segments and the *suggested* times for discussion.

Noting these times will help you as you plan your sessions according to your individual meetings. For instance, if your group meets for two hours, you will likely have enough time to cover most of the questions, and you are welcome to use any extra time to discuss some of the previous week's homework together. Or, if your group meets for 90 minutes, you may need to select which questions you feel will draw your participants into the fullness of the group discussion. Our main goal isn't to "cover" every single question, but to have deeply beneficial discussion times. In our experience, we've learned that some of the most profound moments in a Bible study occur when participants share their own experiential wisdom with one another.

Your group may opt to devote two meetings rather than one to each session. This option allows conversations to more fully explore the content in both the study guide and the book. Where the first meeting could be devoted to watching the teaching video and responding to the group questions, the second meeting could be devoted to exploring the insights gained from the personal study days.

FACILITATION

Having a facilitator for each group helps in numerous ways. A facilitator is responsible for starting the video teachings. Plus, a facilitator can also read the questions aloud, encourage participation, and help keep track of time. A brief leader's guide for each session can be found in the back of this study guide.

Schedule
WEEK 1

BEFORE FIRST GROUP GATHERING	Read the introduction and chapters 1–2 in *Good Boundaries and Goodbyes* book.
FIRST GROUP GATHERING	Watch Video Session 1 Group Discussion Pages 12–21
PERSONAL STUDY DAY 1	Pages 22–27
PERSONAL STUDY DAY 2	Pages 27–33
PERSONAL STUDY DAY 3	Pages 34–40
PERSONAL STUDY DAYS 4 & 5	Read Chapters 3–4 in *Good Boundaries and Goodbyes* book and complete any unfinished personal study activities.

WEEK 1

Boundaries Aren't Just a **Good** Idea, They're a **God** Idea

THIS WEEK'S TRUTH TO HOLD ONTO:

"Boundaries aren't just a good idea, they are a God idea."

WELCOME!

(Suggested Time: 2–5 Minutes)

Welcome to session 1 of *Good Boundaries and Goodbyes*. If this is your first time gathering as a group, take a moment to introduce yourselves to one another before watching the teaching video. Then let's dive in!

OPENING REFLECTION:

(Suggested time: 10–15 minutes)

Leader Note: Before starting the video, have a few people share their responses to this question:

What are you most looking forward to as you begin this study?

VIDEO:

(Running time: 22:00 minutes)

Leader Note: Play the teaching video for the Introduction and Session 1.

VIDEO NOTES:

As you watch the video, use the outline below to help you follow along with the teaching and to take additional notes on anything that stands out to you.

God established the entire universe using boundaries to separate light from darkness, the sea from dry land, and the earth from the heavens.

The purpose of this study on boundaries isn't so that we can shove love away. Quite the opposite. This is so we can know what to do when we very much want to love those all around us really well without losing ourselves in the process.

God's ultimate assignment is for us to love Him and love others.

> **John 13:34–35**
>
> "A new command I give you: Love one another. As I have loved you, so you must love one another. By this everyone will know that you are my disciples, if you love one another."

Love must be honest. Love must be safe. Love must seek each person's highest good. And ultimately love must honor God.

Good boundaries and goodbyes should bring relief to the grief of letting other people's opinions, issues, misplaced desires, and unhealthy agendas run our life.

Trust is the oxygen of all human relationships.

When we allow someone else access to us emotionally, physically, financially, mentally, spiritually, etc. . . . we need to require them to be responsible with that access. If I give someone level 10 access but they are only willing or capable of level 3 responsibility . . . relational tension will exist. Trust will erode. And frustration will be ever increasing.

People who are irresponsible with our hearts should not be granted great access to our hearts.

Three words that can help us better understand the tension that exists in so many of our important relationships are:

- Access
- Responsibility
- Consequences

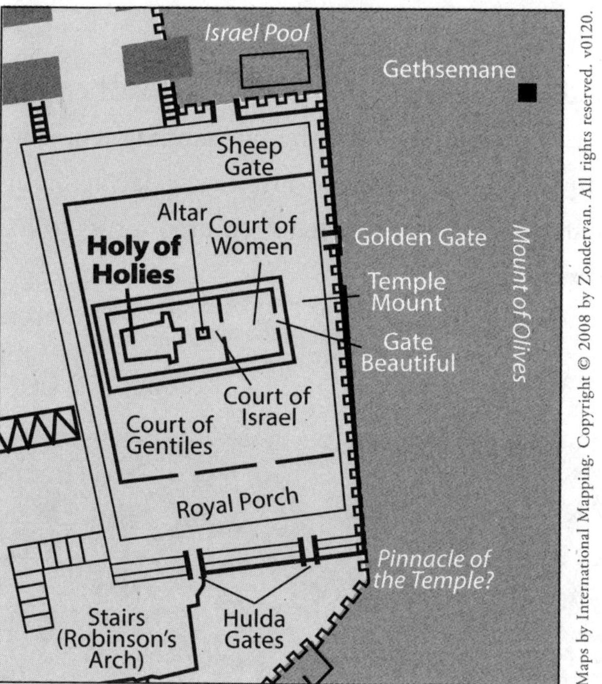

The greater access people had to God, the greater responsibility they had to demonstrate with the requirements for that access. And those given the greatest access also risked the greater consequences for violating those requirements.

Today, Jesus is the forever High Priest. And we (you and I) are the "royal priesthood."

1 Peter 1:22

Now that you have purified yourselves by obeying the truth so that you have sincere love for each other, love one another deeply, from the heart.

Loving each other and treating each other well is not based on fickle feelings or even our mood for that day. . . . Love is shaped by the unchanging truth of God's Word. So think about this: As God gives us great access to Him each day, it should make us all be more responsible and honestly more aware of what's required for us to have access to others and for them to have access to us.

1 Peter 2:9

But you are a chosen people, a royal priesthood, a holy nation, God's special possession, that you may declare the praises of him who called you out of darkness into his wonderful light.

1 Peter 2:17

Show proper respect to everyone, love the family of believers, fear God, honor the emperor.

We don't draw boundaries to shove others away or even to try and make them change. We place boundaries on ourselves, so we can keep ourselves together, so we can be that royal priest God has called us to be.

Group DISCUSSION

(Suggested Time: 40–45 Minutes)

Leader Note: The ultimate goal for this time together is to have a meaningful discussion with others as you grow in your understanding of God's Word. The following suggested questions are designed to guide you through a rich discussion time together. Feel at liberty to select from any of the additional questions as well.

SUGGESTED QUESTIONS . . .

1. When it comes to boundaries, both those you've set and those that have been placed around you, you've likely had a range of experiences. Perhaps some were positive and others less so. Before watching this video, what feelings did you have whenever you thought about boundaries? Circle the following words that best represent how you have felt about boundaries prior to this study. You may circle as many as you like, and it's okay if you have mixed emotions! Then share with your group what you circled.

disappointed	*hopeful*	*curious*	*unsure*	*resentful*
flourishing	*free*	*sad*	*constricted*	*grateful*
skeptical	*used*	*safe*	*exposed*	*frustrated*

2. Please open your Bible and read Psalm 61:1–2. Other common emotions people might feel when talking about boundaries are "exhausted" and "confused." How does this verse encourage and equip you with some of the harder feelings you might have?

3. In today's video, we learned that trust is the oxygen to all human relationships. Why is it important to consider trust in relationships when talking about boundaries?

4. When we are considering the access we give to others, trust is crucial. For example, I doubt any of us would post our bank account information and passwords on social media today. If this is true with bank accounts and other external areas of importance, then it should also be true internally and with relationships. What are some other areas of your life where you have neglected to put protective boundaries in place?

5. When God modeled access and responsibility, such as with the tabernacle which eventually turned into the temple, we need to remind ourselves it's not being done as a penalty or punishment. When you experience boundaries, where does your mind and heart naturally turn to? Why?

6. Read 1 Peter 2:9 aloud: "But you are a chosen people, a royal priesthood, a holy nation, God's special possession, that you may declare the praises of him who called you out of darkness into his wonderful light." Today, you and I are the royal priesthood with access to God's presence. As a group, discuss the four characteristics mentioned in 1 Peter 2:9 and why they are important to the access God has granted to us.

7. Open your Bibles and have a different person in your group each read a passage aloud: John 14:6; Romans 5:1–2; Ephesians 2:13; Hebrews 10:19–22. After reading each passage, discuss the benefits we receive as a result of our access to God. Of the four passages, which one sticks out to you most, and why?

ADDITIONAL QUESTIONS . . .

8. Reflect on this excerpt from today's teaching, then answer the following questions:

   "Here's the mistake I've made—one that honestly I think we've all made—I've tried to put boundaries on the other person, hoping to get them to increase their level of responsibility up to the access I've granted them. But that doesn't really work. You can't make another person change. You can ask them to demonstrate more responsibility, but you can't 'boundary' them into making changes they maybe aren't willing or capable of making. So, the only real productive choice is for you to put boundaries in place that reduce the level of access you give to that person to match their level of responsibility."

When it comes to having healthy boundaries in our lives, this is a powerful paradigm shift. We don't place boundaries on others, we place boundaries on ourselves. And we do this by recognizing the level of responsibility another person has demonstrated and then choosing to give that person the appropriate level of access to our hearts. This isn't stinginess on our parts. This is wisdom. But our past experiences might make us reluctant to practice this effectively in our lives.

Do you feel any reluctance to putting such boundaries in place in your life? If so, what do you think is the reason for your hesitation?

9. We've covered a lot of ground in just this first session already. What is one Bible verse that has stood out to you? Write it in the space below.

10. As you continue to process all you've learned today, spend a few moments writing down any situations, circumstances, or relationships that you want to put before the Lord. Consider returning to this list throughout the week and ask God to give you wisdom and discernment in how you can make the very best decisions to ensure a healthy environment and relationships.

CLOSING: (Suggested time: 5 minutes)

Leader Note: Read the following instructions and clarify any questions your group may have pertaining to the homework and what each participant should do between now and the next session. Then take a few minutes to pray over your group. You may pray either your own prayer or the prayer provided below.

BEFORE THE NEXT SESSION . . .

Every week in the *Good Boundaries and Goodbyes Study Guide* includes five days of personal study to help you draw closer to God as you seek to implement healthy boundaries in your life. For this first week of personal study, you will work with the content in the introduction and chapters 1–2 of the book *Good Boundaries and Goodbyes*. You will also have time to read chapters 3–4 of the book in preparation for our next session together.

PRAYER

Lord, as we begin this journey to learn more about You and the healthy boundaries You prescribe in Scripture, we first want to thank You for being a God who cares so much for each of us that You desire for us to be whole, and the boundaries You have designed lead to wholeness. Forgive us for the times we have resisted Your boundaries and help us to receive Your boundaries as truly life-giving. Grow in us the ability to trust You more and more, especially as we discover what it means to implement healthy boundaries in our own lives. We are in awe of Your amazing goodness, and we give You all our praise. In Jesus' name, amen.

Personal STUDY

DAY 1

Read the Introduction

STUDY AND REFLECT

Hello, friend! I am so glad you are here. Today we're going to reflect more on the introduction of the book *Good Boundaries and Goodbyes*. If you haven't had a chance to read the introduction yet, you'll want to do that now before you begin.

> **"Boundaries protect the right kind of love and help prevent dysfunction from destroying that love." (p. xviii)**

As we begin to explore what the Bible says about boundaries, we want to start, first and foremost, with this truth: good boundaries are not about pushing people away. They're about protecting and preserving what is most beautiful in a healthy relationship.

If we could gather around a table and share our stories in person, every one of us would have a unique story of how boundaries have played a distinctive role in our relationships and our lives. While our circumstances may be different, we are very much the same in the way God has designed our hearts, minds, bodies, and souls to thrive in contexts where healthy boundaries are set in place.

Maybe you've experienced the kind of boundaries that protected your heart and shielded your soul. Or maybe you've known the heartache that comes when boundaries have been broken.

Maybe you've had some success with establishing positive boundaries in your life. Or maybe you've tried implementing boundaries in the past, but somehow it backfired and left you feeling raw and exposed.

Maybe you're a long-time advocate of healthy boundaries in families and friendships. Or maybe you're wondering if such a thing is even possible.

Whatever your previous experiences with boundaries have been, whether super beneficial or painfully disappointing, this study is designed to invite you into a fuller understanding of how God has created this world and every person in it to experience the wholeness that comes from beautiful God-planned boundaries.

1. When it comes to having good boundaries in your relationships, how would you rate yourself when it comes to setting boundaries in your own life?

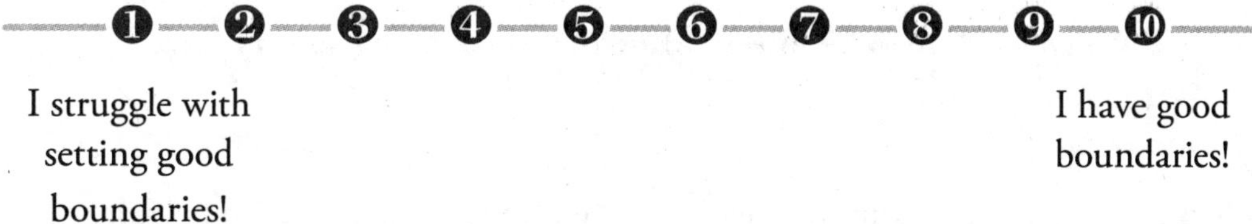

Consider asking a trusted friend or family member to rate you. Compare your responses and discuss.

2. Read 2 Corinthians 9:8: "And God is able to bless you abundantly, so that in all things at all times, having all that you need, you will abound in every good work." God promises to provide us with all we need to abound in every good work. And I think we'd all agree that the effort needed to establish and maintain good relationships is "good work"! How does this verse speak to your heart as you begin the good work of this study?

3. Please read the book excerpt below and then answer the questions that follow.

> **"When we dare to be so very known, we risk being so very hurt." (p. xiv)**

When we open ourselves up to others . . . when we allow ourselves to be vulnerable . . . when we let people into those deeply personal places in our hearts . . . we risk being hurt. This is part of what it means to be human and to navigate our way through human relationships. But sometimes we attribute these human characteristics to God. Deep down, we may wonder if God is going to let us down or somehow not come through. Look up the following passages: Numbers 23:19; Deuteronomy 4:31; 7:9; Psalm 33:4. How does Scripture describe God?

4. Open your Bible and read John 13:34. What is God's assignment for each of us?

5. Good boundaries empower us to love others well. But sometimes we try to love others and we get it wrong and end up hurt. To love others well, we must begin with God's definition of love and not the world's definition. Turn to 1 Corinthians 13:4–7 and read how the Bible defines love. Then in the space below, write an example of when you saw this kind of biblical love in action, whether it was something you did or something someone else did.

6. God's description of real love is not a list for us to use as a weapon against others; rather, it's a list for us to use as a measure of ourselves. For instance, we want to ask ourselves: *Am I patient? Am I kind? Am I envious or boastful? Am I keeping a record of wrongs?* Then we want to ask God to grow us in those areas where we are lacking. Spend a few moments inviting the Holy Spirit to show you one area of love where you need to grow. Then write down one practical way you can practice growing in love this week.

7. Please read the book excerpt below and then answer the questions that follow.

> **"And, remember, we can't set good boundaries without love. Setting boundaries from a place of anger and bitterness will only lead to control and manipulation . . . But setting boundaries from a place of love provides an opportunity for relationships to grow deeply because true connection thrives within the safety of health and honesty." (p. xviii)**

Good boundaries begin from a place of love. They're never used to manipulate. They're meant to create a place of safety, so people can trust that it's okay to be fully present with those around them. What is one way you have experienced or observed someone setting a good and healthy boundary? How did that good boundary help you or others?

8. Sometimes we're afraid to set good boundaries in our lives because we're afraid that others might get angry with us and our boundaries. Then they might withdraw their love from us. But with God, we need never worry about Him withdrawing His love from us as some sort of retaliation maneuver. Read Isaiah 54:10 and Romans 8:38–39. Then highlight or circle the imagery in these verses. What is the imagery and language that the prophet Isaiah uses to describe the love of God? How does Paul in Romans depict the love of God? When you read these two passages, one from the Old Testament and the other from the New Testament, what can you conclude about God's love?

Finish your study time today by writing a prayer of thanks to God for His steadfast love that will never fail you.

Read Chapter 1

I'm not always great at setting healthy boundaries. I'm still learning, too! That's why I am so grateful to be on this journey with you. Every journey is made better when we can make it together. And this business about boundary-making is no small task! We need each other for support along the way.

Good boundaries are essential for healthy, strong relationships. This isn't my idea or someone else's idea; it's God's idea.

> **"[B]oundaries aren't just a good idea, they are a God idea." (p. 7)**

Boundaries have been God's idea since the beginning of time. This will be our focus for today's personal study. We will turn to the earliest pages of Scripture to see some of the ways the Bible describes God as a Boundary-Maker. Not only are boundaries necessary for this planet to be inhabitable, but **boundaries are also crucial for people to experience healthy and vibrant ways of relating to one another.**

If you haven't had a chance yet to read chapter 1 in the book, do that now before completing today's study.

1. Please read the book excerpt below and then answer the questions that follow.

> **"Boundaries are woven into everything God has done since the very beginning . . . God even put an actual boundary around the sea during creation. The sea would eventually be known to the people who lived during biblical times as a symbol of chaos. So, the boundary for the sea was a barrier of sand placed by God that the chaos was not allowed to cross." (pp. 7–8)**

   Let's go back to the creation account in Genesis and dive a little deeper. Open your Bible and read Genesis 1:1–2. For some, this passage may feel familiar, but read it slowly and list the ways the earth is initially described.

   Would it be possible for humans to dwell on the earth as it is described in Genesis 1:2? Why or why not?

2. Now read Genesis 1:3–10 and note how many times this passage of Scripture uses the word "separate" or "separated." Then fill in the following blanks that demonstrate the separations/boundaries that God created. (The following passages are taken from the NIV.)

   God separated the light from the ______________________. (v. 4)

God gathered the ____________________ to one place and let dry ____________________ appear. (v. 9)

God called the dry ground ____________________, and the waters he called ____________________. (v. 10)

3. In order to make this planet inhabitable, God needed to put some boundaries in place. By separating the light from the darkness, *God created a boundary of time* as He differentiated day and night. Then, as He designated the land regions as distinct from the seas, *God created a boundary of space*. So, within the first few verses of Scripture, we see God as a Boundary-Maker. What word does God use to describe the boundaries He has made? (v. 10)

4. Read Genesis 2:16–17. At this point in human history, the first man and woman, Adam and Eve, were enjoying the fruits of the land and the company of God and each other. But in the midst of this garden paradise, what additional boundary did God establish? What would the consequence be if this boundary was crossed?

5. Read the book quote below and then respond to the questions that follow.

> **"Love given is wildly beautiful. Love received is wildly fulfilling. But for love to thrive as true and lasting, it must be within the safety of trust." (pp. 2–3)**

I want to pause right here and acknowledge how brutally devastating it can be when trust is broken in a relationship where you thought you were safe enough to be vulnerable. That's my story, too. And for a season, I started to feel like because that one person wasn't safe, all people weren't safe.

Then there were others who hurt me in the same season and that just compounded my trust issues, even to the point where I sometimes wondered if I could even trust God. One thing that started helping me regain my footing with trusting friends again and even God again was by intentionally listing out some recent actions I've experienced that were good and demonstrated faithfulness.

How have you experienced the goodness of some people recently? How have you experienced some of God's faithfulness recently?

6. Sometimes Christians have some confusion about boundaries. I've listed a few of those wrong notions below. What other wrong thinking would you add to this list?

   - Being a Christian means it's unkind to draw boundaries.
   - Being a Christian means believing the best no matter what.
   - Being a Christian means it's noble to stay in a relationship no matter what.
   - Being a Christian means ____.
   - Being a Christian means ____.
   - Being a Christian means ____.
   - Being a Christian means ____.

   In the margins of this book, go ahead and write, "Wrong thinking!" and then draw an arrow to all the wrong notions listed above.

7. Read Jeremiah 5:22b: "I made the sand a boundary for the sea, an everlasting barrier it cannot cross. The waves may roll, but they cannot prevail; they may roar, but they cannot cross it." God's boundary between the land and the sea is for our protection. The same

is true for boundaries in our personal relationships. Boundaries are like guardrails that protect us from dangerous cliffs. Read the following excerpt from the book and then answer the following question:

> **"Please know: it's not unchristian to set these healthy parameters. It's not unchristian to require people to treat you in healthy ways. And for us to do the same for others. It's not unchristian to call wrong things wrong and hurtful things hurtful. We can do it all with honor, kindness, and love, but we have to know how to spot dysfunction, what to do about it, and when to recognize it's no longer reasonable or safe to stay in some relationships." (p. 8)**

Friends, chaos shouldn't be the norm. Wherever there is chaos, there is a lack of boundaries. Just as God separated the sea—the "chaos"—from the land, sometimes we will be called to separate ourselves from the chaos in our own lives with healthy, appropriate boundaries. Sometimes these separations/boundaries are needed only for a season, and sometimes they're required permanently. We will discuss this in greater detail in the coming pages, but for now, consider any possible areas of "chaos" in your life and ask God to show where you need to grow and possibly change. List below some of these possible areas.

8. As we wrap up today's personal study time, let's review a few of the ways we see God as a Boundary-Maker in the Bible. Circle the one that is *not* true.

    - When God separated light from darkness, He created a boundary of time.
    - When God separated land from water, He created a boundary of space.
    - When God placed a boundary around the tree of the knowledge of good and evil, He wanted to tempt Adam and Eve.
    - When God placed a boundary around the tree of the knowledge of good and evil, He wanted to give Adam and Eve the choice of whether they wanted to be in a trusted relationship with Him or not.

9. Boundaries are God's idea. He is a boundary-making God. But God doesn't set boundaries in place to limit human flourishing or diminish potential fun. Boundaries are beautiful because they create order from disorder, peace from chaos. Read Psalm 16:6. Let the words from this verse be a declaration of praise to God. And if the words from this verse don't feel like a declaration of praise just yet, perhaps pray the words of this verse as a hopeful sacrifice of praise. Then invite God to reveal more of Himself to you during this journey and to show you what it means to proclaim this verse with joy and thanksgiving. Write out your prayer for this new journey in the space below.

Read Chapter 2

As we begin Day 3 together, I want to encourage you in the hard and holy work you are doing. Your commitment to growing healthier in the way you relate to those around you is one of the best ways you can love God and others. **We can't change anyone else, but by God's grace, we can change ourselves.** We can learn to see old relationship patterns from new perspectives. And we can increase our capacity for healthier relationships.

That's what we're here to do. To grow strong, loving, beautiful relationships. With God and with others.

We likely already know which relationships in our lives need "something more," but sometimes we're not sure what that "something more" might be. We haven't been able to put our finger on it or give it a name. We just know something is off, and sometimes it leaves us wondering if we're crazy. Is it me? Is it them? Or is it some combination of both? How can I ever sort it out? Is it even possible to live with peace when this other person in my life is causing so much strife?

Oh, friend, I have asked all of these questions countless times. And I want this study to be a safe place where we can sit with our questions and seek God's Word for answers.

One thing I have learned through the many hours of studying God's Word is this: **Healthy relationships celebrate healthy boundaries.** It's that simple, but it's also very hard. It's hard because we're fallen creatures with a sin-bent nature. But we are not without hope! This will be the focus of today's personal study. We will look more closely at the most important relationship in every person's life. Our relationship with God.

Once you've read chapter 2 in the book *Good Boundaries and Goodbyes*, let's jump right in with today's study!

1. As we saw in yesterday's study, a perfect communion existed between God and the first humans in Genesis 1–2. They enjoyed each other's presence. They shared long talks together. They took pleasure in the creation around them. Everything was perfect. Until it wasn't.

   Read Genesis 3:1–7. What was the first boundary broken in the history of humanity?

2. Read the book quote and then respond as directed below.

   > **"[B]oth sin and iniquity have consequences that change the access God allows in His relationships." (p. 18)**

   List some of the consequences that resulted after Adam and Eve broke God's boundary.

   Consequences for the serpent (Genesis 3:14–15):

   Consequences for Eve (Genesis 3:16):

   Consequences for Adam (Genesis 3:17–19):

   Consequences for all of humanity (Genesis 3:22–24):

3. In Genesis 3 a beautiful relationship—between God and two people—is marred by a broken boundary. And the consequences are both painful and real. Read the following excerpt from the book and then respond to the following questions.

> **"Love can be unconditional but relational access never should be. God loves us but He has established that sin causes separation from Him. When Adam and Eve sinned, they were no longer given the same kind of access." (p. 17)**

In your own words, explain why it was necessary for God to remove Adam and Eve from His presence. What attribute of God is honored by this consequence? Why was this consequence more an act of grace than an act of punishment? See Exodus 33:20; Isaiah 6:3; Hebrews 12:14.

4. To be honest, I used to think it wasn't fair that everyone in the world would have to suffer the consequences of Adam and Eve's boundary-breaking disobedience. But deeply embedded in this consequence for all people is also a grace for all people. Read Romans 5:18–19 and rewrite it below in your own words.

5. Grace. Even as God justly allowed the consequences as a result of Adam and Eve's grave disobedience, He weaves grace into the new fabric of their lives. Let's trace God's grace throughout this same passage of Scripture. How does Genesis 3:15 point to a promise of coming redemption? See Hebrews 2:14; and 1 John 3:8.

6. Grace upon grace. Until the promised redemption could come—when Christ would defeat Satan on the cross once and for all—what did God do for Adam and Eve in the meantime? Read Genesis 3:21. How was this an upgrade from the clothing Adam and Eve had made for themselves? Refer back to Genesis 3:7.

7. While this story in Genesis may feel familiar to many, it's a critical dividing point in history, and it shows us that God is serious about maintaining good and beautiful relationships. It shows us that God isn't willing to deny who He is—He is holy!—and He won't let anyone recklessly disrespect His boundaries. This passage also shows us that God is serious about grace, too. He wants to reconcile with those who have broken His boundaries.

   According to Paul in Romans 3:10 and 3:23, who has broken God's boundaries and suffered the consequences?

   According to John in 1 John 1:9, what can we do when we have been the ones who have sinned?

   According to the wisdom in Proverbs 4:23, what are we called to do as we relate to others?

8. Please read the book quote below and then respond to the questions that follow.

   > **"Setting a boundary is being responsible enough to reduce the access we grant to others based on their ability to be responsible with that access." (p. 21)**

   Can you think of a relationship in your life that has been difficult to the point that it's actually been detrimental to your well-being? Have you ever wondered if you're the crazy one? Do you ever wonder if the problem is hopeless? List some of the ways your well-being has suffered due to boundaries not being honored.

Friend, you may have a relationship in your life where someone has recklessly disrespected or discounted your boundaries that were meant to provide protection and care. Broken boundaries can be life-altering, not only for those who break the boundaries, but also for those who had boundaries shattered against their will. And the cost is devastating for everyone involved. But there's a hope we can hold onto, even in the midst of heart-crushing circumstances, and it's this: **We serve a God who truly understands what we are going through.** He knows what it's like to give and give and give, only to hear His beloved say with their actions, "No thanks. I want something else." Read Isaiah 53:3; Hebrews 4:15; and Psalm 34:18. How do these three verses describe our God? How do these truths shape the way you view God?

9. Read Psalm 34:18 again. Spend a few moments talking to God about your relationship with Him. Confess the ways that you have wrongly crossed the lines He has drawn, as outlined in Scripture, and ask for His forgiveness. (And I will do the same!) Then tell God how grieved you are for the ways your actions have caused Him pain. Ask Him to help you, by the power of His Spirit, to honor the boundaries He has made as you move forward in life. Then take a moment to tell God how a certain relationship in your life has left you feeling. Ask Him to grow in you a vision for biblically healthy boundaries. Write out your prayer in the space below, thanking Him that He is a God who draws near to the brokenhearted and that He saves those who are crushed in spirit.

DAY 4 & 5

Read Chapters 3–4

REVIEW AND READ

Use this time to go back and complete any of the reflection questions or activities from previous days this week that you weren't able to finish. Make note of any revelations you've had and reflect on any growth or personal insights you've gained.

Spend the next two days reading chapters 3 and 4 in the book *Good Boundaries and Goodbyes*. Use the space below to make note of anything in the chapters that stands out to you or encourages your heart.

Schedule
WEEK 2

BEFORE GROUP GATHERING	Read chapters 3–4 in *Good Boundaries and Goodbyes* book
GROUP GATHERING	Watch Video Session 2 Group Discussion Pages 44–53
PERSONAL STUDY DAY 1	Pages 54–57
PERSONAL STUDY DAY 2	Pages 58–62
PERSONAL STUDY DAY 3	Pages 63–68
PERSONAL STUDY DAYS 4 & 5	Read Chapters 5–6 in *Good Boundaries and Goodbyes* book and complete any unfinished personal study activities

WEEK 2

A **Relationship** Can Only Be as **Healthy** as the **People** in It

THIS WEEK'S TRUTH TO HOLD ONTO:

"A relationship can only be as healthy as the people in the relationship."

WELCOME AND OPENING REFLECTION:

(Suggested time: 15–20 minutes)

Welcome to session 2 of *Good Boundaries and Goodbyes.*

Leader Note: Have a few people share their response to this question before starting the video:

What was your most helpful takeaway from this week's homework?

VIDEO:

(Running time: 28:00 minutes)

Leader Note: Play the video segment for session 2.

VIDEO NOTES:

Use the outline below to help you follow along with the teaching video and to take additional notes on anything that stands out to you.

Better small decisions lead to better habits. Better habits lead to positive changes.

If we want more peaceful relationships, we have to turn our life from accepting chaos to pursuing peace.

If we want to . . . know what to look for to determine if our relationships are healthy or unhealthy, a great place to turn to is the book of Proverbs.

Since it's really hard to see someone's heart, why don't we start with what we can see: the choices that they make.

Knowledge → Information necessary for wisdom

Discernment → Being able to process that information rightly

Consideration → Thinking about how actions will affect other people

Application → Following through on doing the right thing

Proverbs 1:7

The fear of the Lord is the beginning of knowledge,
but fools despise wisdom and instruction.

As we pay attention to choices, we have to remember to first examine ourselves—our actions and our reactions.

Proverbs 12:15

The way of fools seems right to them,
but the wise listen to advice.

Proverbs 3:7

Do not be wise in your own eyes;
fear the Lord and shun evil.

Proverbs 14:15b

. . . the prudent give thought to their steps.

If we refuse wisdom in our relationships or if we ignore red flags when someone in our lives has a pattern of unwise choices, it will be especially painful when times of trouble come our way.

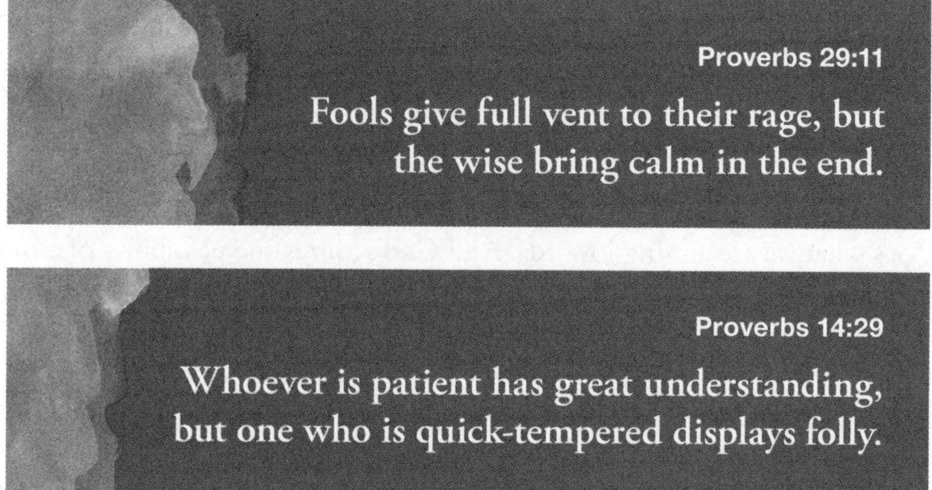

As we think through all of these Proverbs and look at how a person uses or rejects knowledge, discernment, consideration, and application, we have to remember this isn't to categorize people . . . This is so we can pursue healthy relationships instead of relationships that cause us harm and suffering.

Proverbs 13:20

Walk with the wise and become wise, for a companion of fools suffers harm.

A relationship can only be as healthy as the people in the relationship.

GOOD WORDS TO REMEMBER:

All verses have a context, and the context is a type of boundary, a type of guardrail, to help us understand the verse the way it was intended. If we take a verse out of context it's so easy to weaponize that verse. – Dr. Joel Muddamalle

Even a separation, or a goodbye, with someone actually has an end goal. The Greek word is "telos," it's what we are aiming towards. And God's aim is the possibility of a future reconciliation, maybe not person to person, but always person to God. – Dr. Joel Muddamalle

Believe and trust that what you see, is what you see. – Jim Cress

Don't make any excuses or explanations for what you see in the life of the other person. . . . This is not helpful to that person. – Jim Cress

If they don't go to the impact, I'm convinced they'll never get to repentance. – Jim Cress

To get free access to a bonus session where we continue this conversation with Lysa, Jim and Joel go to PROVERBS31.ORG/BOUNDARIES-EXTRAS

Group DISCUSSION

(Suggested Time: 40–45 Minutes)

Leader Note: We have suggested questions to start with, but feel free to pick any of the additional questions as well. Consider the timeframe of your group and know the ultimate goal is meaningful discussion.

SUGGESTED QUESTIONS . . .

1. In today's teaching, we learned that a wise person makes choices that lead toward order and away from chaos. What are some examples you can think of where seemingly small actions or habits lead to positive gains over time? Share your response with your group.

2. In the Video Notes from today's teaching, several passages from the book of Proverbs are given. Have each person in your group take one or two of the passages; then work together as a group to create a list of words that describe a wise person and a foolish person. Use the two columns below to record your answers.

Wise Person	Foolish Person

3. Open your Bible and read James 3:13–17. From this passage, what might you add to the list above?

4. It's always wise to honestly evaluate ourselves first. As you review the descriptions listed in question 2, which ones best describe you, and in which areas would you like to see personal growth? Why?

5. According to James 3:18, who will reap a harvest of righteousness? How do healthy boundaries foster peace-filled relationships?

ADDITIONAL QUESTIONS . . .

6. In today's video, Joel describes the practice of biblical discernment versus judgment. Read Luke 6:37; 1 Corinthians 5:12–13; Hebrews 5:14; and Philippians 1:9–10. In your own words, how would you describe discernment as different from judgment? Why is exercising biblical discernment part of a wise person's life?

7. Based on the group discussion in the video, what can you do when you recognize unhealthy patterns in one of your relationships?

8. What is your biggest takeaway from today's video discussion with Joel and Jim? Share with the group.

CLOSING: (Suggested time: 5 minutes)

Leader Note: End your session by reading the "Between-Sessions Personal Studies" instructions below to the group and ask if there are any questions pertaining to the homework. Then take a few minutes to pray over your group, either reading the provided prayer aloud over them or praying your own prayer.

BETWEEN-SESSIONS PERSONAL STUDIES . . .

Every week in the *Good Boundaries and Goodbyes Study Guide* includes five days of personal study to help you make meaningful connections between your life and what you're learning each week. This week, you'll work with the material in chapters 3–4 of the book *Good Boundaries and Goodbyes*. You'll also have time to read chapters 5–6 of the book in preparation for our next session together.

PRAYER

Lord, we truly desire to be people who pursue wisdom. Help us to look to You and Your Word to grow in wisdom. And as we go about our daily lives, help us to make better choices in even the small things we face, because we know that better actions lead to positive changes. On our own we are powerless, but You are a mighty God and the same power that raised Christ from the dead now lives in us. May we look to You as the source of our strength, trusting that You will accomplish in us all that You desire. We love You and praise You, for You are a magnificent God. In Jesus' name we pray, amen.

Personal STUDY

DAY 1

Today we're going to spend a little more time reflecting on this week's video teaching on wisdom versus foolishness. Since relationships are only as healthy as the people in them, it's of great importance that we grow in wisdom so we can establish good boundaries that foster healthy relationships.

What makes some people wise and other people foolish? What does the Bible have to say about wisdom? How can I become a person of wisdom? We will discuss these topics and more today and in the days to come.

Here's a quick look at this week's personal study days:

In Day 1, we'll talk about how the wise react well.

In Day 2, we'll discuss how the wise have hard conversations.

In Day 3, we'll explore how the wise guard the gateways to life.

Today, we will focus on reactions.

"A key indicator of either wisdom or folly is found in someone's reactions."

While we cannot always choose what happens to us, we can always choose how we will respond to the situations around us. And our choices reveal what is inside our hearts. Since we have a much better chance at having healthy relationships when our hearts are healthy, let's examine our reactions and our hearts . . .

1. For today's study time, we will compare and contrast the reactions of two prominent biblical figures: Judah and Joseph. Read Genesis 38:1–24. What is Judah's reaction when he discovers Tamar is pregnant and unmarried? How does Judah's reaction reveal what is in his heart?

2. Now turn in your Bible and read Matthew 1:18–19. What is Joseph's reaction when he discovers that his fiancé, Mary, is pregnant and unmarried? How does Joseph's reaction reveal what is in his heart?

3. These stories might seem extreme, but they exemplify how our hearts drive our actions and our reactions. Undoubtedly, we've all reacted to situations in ways we wish we could take back, but with God there is always hope for our hearts when we are worn and weary. Read Genesis 38:25–26. How did Judah's heart change once he learned the truth regarding his own culpability in Tamar's situation?

4. Read Ezekiel 36:26 and fill in the blanks below. (The following passage is taken from the NIV.)

   "I will give you a new ______________ and put a new ______________ in you; I will remove from you your heart of ____________________ and give you a heart of __________."

   Why does God's promise here give us great hope?

5. Ultimately, God restored Judah and used him in a significant way. Read the prophetic blessing in Genesis 49:1, 8–11 and the fulfillment of that blessing in the genealogy in Matthew 1:1–3. (Note: A prophetic blessing is a promise from God of good that will come in the future.) What key role did Judah play in the grand story of God's redemption?

6. Read Proverbs 2:6. Where does wisdom come from? Now read Proverbs 2:1–5. How can we grow in wisdom?

7. What warning are we given in Ephesians 5:15–16? What is one practical way you can live this out in your everyday life?

8. Friend, we serve a God who purposes to give us new hearts, so we can live wisely and respond to situations with wisdom and grace. In the space below, write about a situation that you are currently facing and ask God to begin the process of changing your heart so you can respond with wisdom and grace.

Read Chapter 3

Today we're going to dive into chapter 3 of the book *Good Boundaries and Goodbyes*. If you haven't already read chapter 3, please do so before you begin.

1. Please read the book excerpt below and answer the question that follows.

> **"Conversations open the way for us to address what is and isn't working. But even more, they help us establish healthy patterns instead of accepting patterns that are unhealthy." (p. 27)**

Sometimes we're hesitant to have hard conversations because we're afraid of the outcome. What if the person we approach rejects our concerns? Or even worse, what if they reject us for bringing them up? The truth is, none of us will do this perfectly, but with God's grace, we can learn to have those necessary conversations in healthy, God-honoring ways. Before starting this study, how would you rate yourself in terms of confidence when it comes to approaching someone you care about with a concern you have?

Terrified! Confident!

2. As we unpack the wisdom in having hard conversations, let's examine an account from Scripture. Read 1 Samuel 25:1–17. How does Scripture describe Abigail? How does Scripture describe Nabal?

3. Please read the book excerpt below and answer the questions that follow.

> **"Distortions of reality feed dysfunctions." (p. 30)**

How was Nabal's view of David and his men a distortion of reality? What was the accurate version of reality? Compare 1 Samuel 25:10–11 with 1 Samuel 25:14–16.

4. Now look at 1 Samuel 25:12–13, 21–22. What consequences were Nabal and his entire household going to face due to Nabal's distortion of reality?

5. Please read the book excerpt below and answer the questions that follow.

> **"Appropriately addressing the issue is healthy. Ignoring the issue increases the likelihood of dysfunction." (p. 30)**

Read 1 Samuel 25:18–35. After hearing the servant's account (1 Samuel 25:17), how did Abigail address this issue?

a. Abigail ignored the situation, thinking it would just go away.

b. Abigail rushed to her husband and pleaded with him to make things right with David.

c. Abigail gathered food for herself and made a fast getaway on a horse to save herself.

d. Abigail set out to have a hard conversation with David, though she knew it could bring her immediate death. To save her entire household, she brought gifts of food to David and asked for his forgiveness.

6. What comes to mind when you hear the word "dysfunction"? Please read the book excerpt below and answer the questions that follow.

> **"Saying 'dysfunction' used to feel so offensive it immediately put me on the defensive. But now, I've learned to simply let it sit in front of me, to tilt my head and dare myself to consider some things. Confession: I have dysfunctions. Other people I know have dysfunctions. Alive humans have dysfunctions. It shouldn't scare us when we acknowledge that dysfunctions exist. But we should be concerned when someone lives as if dysfunctions are normal." (p. 28)**

How would you define dysfunction?

Is it challenging to consider the idea that, as sin-stained humans, we've all experienced dysfunction to a degree? How does the Bible point us to hope? Read Romans 8:23–25.

7. Part of the problem with dysfunction is it can begin to feel normal when we've been living with it for a long time. (Hello, floodlights and hot water!) But deep down, we often sense something is amiss, we just might not have the words yet to describe what we're sensing. Can you think of a relationship that isn't functioning quite as it should be?

   Prayerfully consider some possible ways where the access you have given someone exceeds the level of responsibility they have demonstrated toward you. Write your thoughts below.

8. Please read the book excerpt below and answer the question that follows.

> **"You get to communicate what makes you feel respected and dis-respected; safe and unsafe; healthy and unhealthy. Your definition of this determines what you need from your closest people." (p. 32)**

If you were to have an honest conversation with the person you identified in question 7, what kinds of things might you need to communicate?

9. Today we saw in Scripture how a woman named Abigail was wise and discerning. And we definitely want to grow in wisdom and discernment. Look up James 1:5 and fill in the blanks below. (The following passage is taken from the NIV.)

"If any of you lacks ________________, you should ________________ God, who gives generously to all without ________________, and it will be ________________ to you."

Finish your personal study time today asking God to grow in you greater wisdom and discernment, and to show you one honest conversation you might need to have.

Read Chapter 4

Today we're going to explore chapter 4 of the book *Good Boundaries and Goodbyes*. If you haven't already read chapter 4, please do so before you begin.

1. Please read the book excerpt below and answer the questions that follow.

> **"So, like I said, sometimes boundaries don't work—because of me and my approach. It's important for me to own this and then do the hard work of changing the way I think about boundaries. And this *is* hard work. It's worthy work, but it isn't easy. If you relate to any of the above, I want to fully acknowledge along with you that all of this can sound much tidier to read about than to actually apply. That's why throughout this journey we need to keep remembering that *good* boundaries originated with God and are modeled by God." (p. 43)**

On Day 3 of Week 1, we studied the consequences that Adam and Eve experienced as a result of their disobedience. We're going to return to that moment in time to examine one additional detail that is key to our personal study today. Read Genesis 3:22–24. When God expelled Adam and Eve from the garden of Eden, what did He place between the people and the garden?

What was God's purpose in doing this?

How was this an act of kindness toward them?

2. Now look up Numbers 3:38; 18:7; and Leviticus 16:1–2. Why was it important for the priests to guard the access into God's presence inside the sanctuary-tabernacle? Were the guards there to punish people or to protect people?

3. Please read the book excerpt below and answer the questions that follow.

> **"They were guards and protectors of the sacred space that God gave them. The same is true of us. We are to guard and protect our hearts and our minds to make sure we keep good in and evil out. We are to guard and protect our testimony and make sure our lives produce the fruit of God's Spirit in us." (p. 44)**

Look up each of the following verses and then answer the corresponding question.

- Read Philippians 1:27–28 and 1 Peter 3:15. What is the testimony we are to guard and protect?

- Read Revelation 12:11. What do our testimonies accomplish because of Christ's blood?

- Read Psalm 119:111 (in the ESV). How does God feel about our testimonies?

4. Guards are important. They protect people and other things of great value. Read Nehemiah 1:1–4. What news did Nehemiah hear about his beloved "hometown" of Jerusalem? What did this mean for the people of Jerusalem? How did Nehemiah initially respond to the news?

Friend, it's okay to weep when appropriate boundaries have been destroyed. God understands our pain. But notice also what Nehemiah did next. Look at Nehemiah 1:4, 6, 11. What one word stands out in these three verses? How does Nehemiah demonstrate wisdom in his response?

Now Read Nehemiah 2:1–8. In addition to being a man of prayer, how else was Nehemiah a man of purposeful action? What did he set out to do?

5. Please read the book excerpt below and answer the questions that follow.

> **"I know I've said it before, and I'll probably say it many more times (mostly because I have to preach this to my Pollyanna self a lot!)—drawing wise boundaries is me fighting for the relationship. It's for their good and mine!" (p. 49)**

Drawing wise boundaries is how we work hard to guard and protect the relationships in our lives. It's not always easy. But when done appropriately it is good. Before Nehemiah set out to rebuild the walls and gates of Jerusalem, what did he wisely do? Read Nehemiah 2:11–16. Why was this important to his task?

In a similar way, we want to emulate Nehemiah by first seeking God in prayer and then purposefully examining the areas in our lives where the boundaries have been broken. This is how we begin to work in positive ways for the relationship, for their good and yours! Spend some time prayerfully asking God to show you where the boundaries in a certain relationship have been broken. What is God showing you?

6. Please read the book excerpt below and answer the questions that follow.

> **"When we allow a boundary to be violated, bad behavior will be validated." (p. 42)**

We never want to validate bad behavior. This is why good boundaries require appropriate consequences. Just as God needed to place guards to the tree of life and guards to the sanctuary-tabernacle, we need to place certain guards in our lives along with appropriate consequences if those boundaries are violated.

To help us sift through the difference between good boundaries and bad boundaries, let's refer to my wise counselor's distinctions on pages 53–56 of the book.

After reviewing some of the distinctions between good and bad boundaries, what is one thing you need to guard and protect? In other words, what is one good boundary you might need to implement in your life today?

What will the natural consequences be if that boundary is broken?

How will you move forward in having that hard conversation to communicate your good boundary?

7. As we close our personal study time today, let's remember this truth:

> **"[B]oundaries aren't going to fix the other person. But they are going to help you stay fixed on what is good, what is acceptable, and what you need to stay healthy and safe." (p. 51)**

Spend a few minutes writing out a prayer of praise for the way God models good boundaries for us. Thank Him for the wisdom He lavishly bestows upon His children. And ask Him to continue to guide you as you purposefully seek to grow healthier in your relationships.

Read Chapters 5–6

REVIEW AND READ

Use this time to go back and complete any of the reflection questions or activities from previous days this week that you weren't able to finish. Make note of any revelations you've had and reflect on any growth or personal insights you've gained.

Spend the next two days reading chapters 5 and 6 in the book *Good Boundaries and Goodbyes.* Use the space below to make note of anything in the chapters that stands out to you or encourages your heart.

Schedule
WEEK 3

BEFORE GROUP GATHERING	Read chapters 5–6 in *Good Boundaries and Goodbyes* book.
GROUP GATHERING	Watch Video Session 3 Group Discussion Pages 72–80
PERSONAL STUDY DAY 1	Pages 81–86
PERSONAL STUDY DAY 2	Pages 86–91
PERSONAL STUDY DAY 3	Pages 92–97
PERSONAL STUDY DAYS 4 & 5	Read Chapters 7–9 in *Good Boundaries and Goodbyes* book and complete any unfinished personal study activities.

WEEK 3

Maybe We've Been Looking at **Walls** All **Wrong**

THIS WEEK'S TRUTH TO HOLD ONTO:

"We aren't talking about building walls to keep others out of our lives. . . . We are talking about boundaries we put on ourselves to help us maintain the self-control we should have as responsible humans and followers of Jesus."

WELCOME AND OPENING REFLECTION:

(Suggested time: 15–20 minutes)

Welcome to session 3 of *Good Boundaries and Goodbyes*.

Leader Note: Have a few people share their responses to this question before starting the video:

What was your most helpful takeaway from this week's homework?

VIDEO:

(Running time: 20:30 minutes)

Leader Note: Play the video segment for session 3.

VIDEO NOTES:

Use the outline below to help you follow along with the teaching video and to take additional notes on anything that stands out to you.

We might have a wall up with someone in our life because it feels like a necessary protection for us. But, taken to an extreme, you can begin to allow that one situation to taint how you see all people as unsafe. . . . The other extreme is to have no walls, no boundaries, and allow everyone 100% access to you at all times. Neither of these extremes work.

Ecclesiastes 7:18b

"Whoever fears God will avoid all extremes."

Boundaries allow for you to communicate what is and is not acceptable.

Boundaries are what give relationships a fighting chance to flourish in agreed upon freedoms.

What if we've been thinking of walls all wrong? What if we've mostly only experienced the extremes of what emotional walls create in us and in others?

There's never a wall built without a gate. There's never a wall built without a watchtower and a watchman on guard.

Nehemiah 1:3b–4a

"…The wall of Jerusalem is broken down, and its gates have been burned with fire." When I heard these things, I sat down and wept.

Exodus 14:22 (ESV)

And the people of Israel went into the midst of the sea on dry ground, the waters being a wall to them on their right hand and on their left.

Proverbs 25:28 (NLT)

A person without self-control is like a city with broken-down walls.

Isaiah 56:10

Israel's watchmen are blind, they all lack knowledge; they are all mute dogs, they cannot bark; they lie around and dream, they love to sleep.

The watchman was trained to know the difference between an unsafe adversary approaching the city and a trusted ally. We must do the same as well.

Psalm 127:1b (ESV)

. . . Unless the LORD watches over the city,
the watchman stays awake in vain.

For me to have limits isn't because I'm selfish. It's because I'm human.

Boundaries shouldn't be used to "peace out" or tap out with fulfilling our roles and responsibilities.

Sometimes the most vulnerable part is also the most necessary part.

Group DISCUSSION

(Suggested Time: 40–45 Minutes)

Leader Note: We have suggested questions to start with, but feel free to pick any of the additional questions as well. Consider the timeframe of your group and know the ultimate goal is meaningful discussion.

SUGGESTED QUESTIONS . . .

1. In biblical times a city was often fortified by a wall with a few gates that allowed friends to visit and merchants to conduct business. Watchmen usually kept vigil atop tall towers that were built into the wall of the city. What were some of the functions of a watchman? Look up each of the following verses for your responses: 2 Samuel 18:24–27; Ezekiel 33:6; Jeremiah 6:17; Proverbs 8:34.

2. Using the same four passages of Scripture from the previous question, answer the following: What are some of the potential consequences if the watchmen fail to uphold their duties? What are some of the potential consequences if the people fail to listen to the watchmen's warnings?

3. Healthy relationships have healthy boundaries, which function like good walls with working gates. Our job as the "watchman" over our own lives is to avoid the two extremes of having either 1) walls with no gates (keeping everyone out, even those who wish us well) or 2) no walls at all (letting even harmful people in). To which of these extremes are you more prone? How might learning about establishing healthy boundaries help? Share your thoughts with the group.

4. Let's examine the "walls" and "gates" we have in our lives. One of the ways we do this is by wisely considering our capacities. Given the season you are currently in, how would you rate your capacity in each of the following areas? Circle the word that best describes your capacity levels right now.

Time/Energy	HIGH — AVERAGE — LOW
Emotions/Feelings	HIGH — AVERAGE — LOW
Finances/Possessions	HIGH — AVERAGE — LOW
Body/Physical Closeness	HIGH — AVERAGE — LOW
Beliefs/Thoughts	HIGH — AVERAGE — LOW

This simple exercise helps us to see more clearly where we may need to "guard" our capacities as wise watchmen over our own lives. Based on the words you circled, where do you see greater capacity, which may indicate the possibility of welcoming new opportunities or more commitments? And where do you see less capacity which may indicate the need to draw some boundaries and say a wise "no" or "not right now"?

5. Reflect on this quote from today's teaching and then answer the following questions:

> **"Remember, only God is limitless. For me to have limits isn't because I'm selfish. It's because I'm human."**

How do Psalm 86:15 and Isaiah 40:28 describe God?

How does Psalm 103:14 describe humanity?

How might these three verses give you assurance that it is, indeed, wise for God's children to have good boundaries in their lives to protect their capacities? How might these verses also give you additional understanding when someone has to say "no" or "not right now" to something you may want from them?

ADDITIONAL QUESTIONS . . .

6. How is God described in Genesis 16:13 and 28:15? What is God seen doing in Deuteronomy 2:7 and Psalm 121:3–4? Why do these Scripture passages bring comfort, peace, and hope?

7. What is one area of your life where you feel you need healthier "walls" or boundaries? Write a short prayer, inviting God into that area of your life, knowing that He never sleeps nor slumbers. God is not asleep on the job!

CLOSING: (Suggested time: 5 minutes)

Leader Note: End your session by reading the "Between-Sessions Personal Studies" instructions to the group and making sure there are no questions pertaining to the homework. Then take a few minutes to pray over your group, either reading the provided prayer aloud over them or praying your own prayer.

BETWEEN-SESSIONS PERSONAL STUDIES . . .

Every week in the *Good Boundaries and Goodbyes Study Guide* includes five days of personal study to help you make meaningful connections between your life and what you're learning each week. This week, you'll work with the material in chapters 5–6 of the book *Good Boundaries and Goodbyes*. You'll also have time to read chapters 7–9 of the book in preparation for our next session together.

PRAYER

Lord, thank You for being the Great Watchman over our lives. We know that You always desire what is best for us, and we are so grateful. We can rest fully, knowing You are never asleep on the job. Help us to wisely follow in Your footsteps as we prayerfully examine the areas in our lives where we may need stronger "walls" and working "gates." We ask for Your wisdom and grace as we grow in our ability to honor our limited capacities while also saying yes to the right requests. Help us to walk in peace as we begin to humbly implement good boundaries in healthy ways so we can love You and love others with the best of who we are. We ask these things in Jesus' name, amen.

Personal STUDY

Read Chapter 5

Friend, I am so proud of how far you have already come in this journey. It's not always easy, I know. There may be some people in your life, and mine, who never see your boundaries as good or helpful. But you are doing the hard work of looking to God in His Word as your example, and that, my friend, is where growth always happens.

Today we're going to examine chapter 5 of the book *Good Boundaries and Goodbyes*. If you haven't already read chapter 5, please do so before you begin.

1. Please read the book excerpt below and answer the question that follows.

> **"You are a responsible person. You want to be a good steward of what's been entrusted to you. Therefore, you walk in reality instead of wishful thinking. You acknowledge and respect the concept of limitations because you don't like how you act and react when you get stretched too thin. And you wisely establish boundaries when people keep pushing for you to go past your capacity. When people aren't respectful of our limits, we can set boundaries, or we can pay consequences." (p. 62)**

Consequences. They're a fact of life. And they work like this: When I don't have good boundaries, I suffer the consequences. When I do have good boundaries, I can better hold together, by God's grace, my sanity and sense of safety. This is crucial because when I am in a good place, I can love others better. When I am depleted and exhausted, I cannot love others well. In what ways have you experienced a feeling of exhaustion, whether physically or emotionally or both, due to a lack of good boundaries?

2. Have you noticed a connection between your emotional stress and your physical stress? How does your emotional stress tend to manifest itself physically in your body?

3. Open your Bible and read Philippians 4:6. Fill in the blanks below. (The following passage is taken from the NIV.)

   "Do _____ be _______________ about _______________ , but in every situation, by prayer and petition, with ________________________, present your _______________ to God."

   What is Paul commanding in this passage?

Based on this one isolated verse, it's tempting to think that it might somehow be "wrong" to be anxious. But read Philippians 2:28. Then fill in the blanks below. (The following passage is taken from the NIV.)

"Therefore I am all the more __________ to send [Epaphroditus], so that when you see him again you may be _______ and I may have less _________________."

Paul freely admits to having anxiety, because it's not necessarily wrong to have anxiety. But the presence of anxiety does serve to indicate that something is triggering us, and it is wise to discern what that is. For Paul, he wanted his friends back in Philippi to see Epaphroditus again, especially since he had recently been ill to the point of almost dying (Philippians 2:29–30).

None of us enjoy having anxiety. But sometimes it's a part of life. In fact, God designed our bodies to use anxiety in moments of danger to prompt us to react quickly so we can return to a place of safety. And yet, the enemy of our souls wants us to hide in shame the fact that we sometimes experience anxiety. How does Paul's admission in Philippians 2:28 dispel the idea that anxiety by itself is somehow wrong or sinful?

4. Please read the book excerpt below and answer the questions that follow.

> **". . . Paul is not saying that we shouldn't be concerned or that we shouldn't acknowledge our troubles. And I especially appreciate that he doesn't tell us to be silent about our troubles. We sometimes need others to help us process and navigate the hardships we are facing. But what Paul is teaching us in Philippians 4:4–9 is what to do when anxiety gets triggered in us" (p. 69)**

One of the keys to understanding Scripture is to take in the fuller context of passages. So, let's take more of a wide-angle lens on this passage in Philippians. Read Philippians 4:4–9. Then circle in your Bible the imperative verbs—the words that give a direct command.

In this passage, Paul is showing us what we can do when we are feeling anxious. Select below the one command that is not in Philippians 4:4–9:

a. Rejoice in the Lord always.

b. Let your gentleness be evident to all.

c. Do not reveal your anxiety to anybody.

d. Present your requests to God.

e. Think about excellent and praiseworthy things.

5. Read Proverbs 15:1 and Colossians 4:6. How do these verses instruct you to communicate your boundaries?

6. Counselor Jim Cress explains that "*Dysregulation* is when an external trigger causes you to go into your limbic system (fight, flight, or freeze mode), which is an automatic physical response to a perceived threat" (p. 77). Whenever you are in a situation where you are feeling threatened either physically or emotionally, what is your common response? Fight, flight, or freeze?

When are these responses to imminent danger considered wise and healthy?

When are they considered unwise and unhealthy?

7. When your limbic system is alerting you to possible danger, below are some helpful tips for when you are feeling triggered. What else would you add to this list?

- Go for a walk.
- Drink some water.
- Give yourself a space of time before responding.
- Be gracious with yourself.
- ______________________________
- ______________________________
- ______________________________
- ______________________________

8. Finish your personal study time today by writing a prayer, thanking God for designing your brain to help you whenever you are facing a very difficult situation, and asking Him to help you respond in ways that are healthy and helpful.

Read Chapter 6

Today we're going to explore chapter 6 of the book *Good Boundaries and Goodbyes.* If you haven't already read chapter 6, please do so before you begin.

1. Please read the book excerpt below and answer the questions that follow.

> **"As I mentioned before, some of the people in my life were on the same journey of growing emotionally and spiritually. But others were not. And as I continued to pursue progress over time, it only exposed the major differences between healthy behaviors and unhealthy ones. It almost started to seem as if some people in my life were more and more offended by my efforts . . ." (pp. 84–85)**

The people who love you and want to see you grow and thrive and become the person God created you to be will be your biggest cheerleaders. They'll be so glad to see the efforts you are making and the positive changes you are implementing. They will want to support you in any way they can.

But there will be some who feel intimidated or possibly offended by your growth, and they may try to impede it. There is even biblical precedent for this. Remember last week when we saw Nehemiah weep at the news of the broken walls in Jerusalem and then gain permission from the king to go and repair the walls? Read Nehemiah 4:6–9. What happened when Nehemiah began construction on those walls?

How did Sanballat, Tobiah, and other neighbors react when they heard that repairs to Jerusalem's walls had begun?

2. How did Nehemiah and the Jews respond to their threat? Read Nehemiah 4:13–20.

3. While the Jewish people held spears and strapped on swords as they worked on the wall, who did they believe would ultimately be their deliverer?

Read again Nehemiah 4:20. How is this significant as you and I go about our daily lives, doing the hard work of establishing boundaries while not always receiving the support of some people around us?

4. Look up Exodus 14:14; Deuteronomy 20:4; and 2 Chronicles 20:17. How is God described in these verses? How have you seen this characteristic of God evident in your own life?

5. Lest we think this is true only of our God in the Old Testament, how has Jesus fought and battled death on our behalf? Read Colossians 2:15 and Hebrews 2:14.

6. Please read the book excerpt below and answer the questions that follow.

> **"And when you decide to establish boundaries and the other person tries to label you as controlling, difficult, or uncooperative, see it as a compliment. Yes, you read that right—see it as a compliment. They are frustrated with you because you are no longer willing to participate in the unhealthy patterns of the past. You have decided to raise your actions and words to higher levels of maturity. And if someone chooses not to join you, there will be great tension. In every relationship there are patterns of relating. If you change the pattern and the other person doesn't agree with the change, there will be agitation. The tension exists because you are doing the difficult work of no longer cooperating with dysfunction." (p. 86)**

In Nehemiah's day, as long as the walls of Jerusalem lay in ruins, the enemies who surrounded Israel felt powerful. Everyone understood that the Jewish inhabitants did not have proper protective boundaries, like a fortified wall, around the city! So, when construction began, the surrounding enemies felt threatened, and they responded with threats and bullying tactics. Such opposition is sometimes par for the course, and it can, at times, be an indicator that we are on the right path.

What does Peter have to say about this in his letter in 1 Peter 4:12–13? How does he instruct us to respond?

7. Please read the book excerpt below and answer the question that follows.

> **"Grieve someone's refusal to keep growing, but don't beg them to see your boundaries as a good thing. They may never see your boundaries as a good thing. Your light exposes something inside of them they'd rather keep hidden in the darkness. So, of course, it's offensive to them." (p. 86)**

Can you think of a relationship in your life where you are experiencing resistance as you begin to implement healthy boundaries? Write your thoughts below.

8. The best way to keep growing is to continuously seek God and ask Him to examine our hearts. With open hands we want to come before Him and let His Spirit convict us where necessary and lead us in the way everlasting. To finish your personal study time, read Psalm 19, giving special attention to verses 12–14, and make it your prayer today.

DAY 3

As we wrap up our study this week on the benefits of walls, gates, and watchmen—both in Scripture as well as in our own lives—let's take one last tour around the city perimeter of ancient Jerusalem. There is so much for us to learn, and it's fascinating!

The gates gave access to specific areas of the city based on function and use. Not only did each gate serve an important function in the city, but each gate also told a story. And it's a story that you and I are a part of!

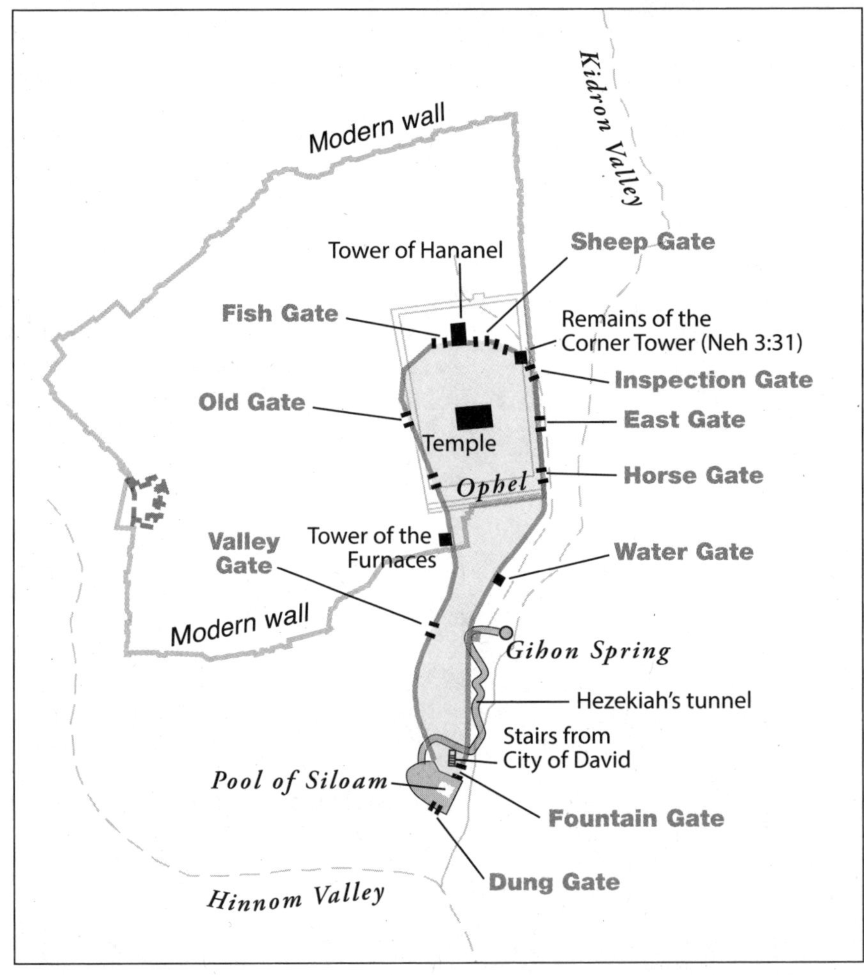

1. Please read the book excerpt below and answer the questions that follow.

> **"Sometimes we feel the pain of setting a boundary and that can make us forget the good reasons we're setting boundaries . . . boundaries are beneficial for both parties in the relationship. So, let's remember that there is also the benefit of what a boundary will do for us personally." (p. 74)**

This boundary-making business is no easy task. There will be ups and downs. And sometimes there will be really hard days. But the task before us is worth every bit of effort involved. Something incredibly beautiful is being forged in the fire of every ordeal we endure when we surrender everything to Jesus. You see, when you do the work of building healthy relationships with God and others, then you have a renewed testimony that was forged in the furnace of life. Last week we talked about being guards of our testimony, and this week I want you to see how the restored "gates" in our lives can serve to tell a story of God's goodness. It was true for Nehemiah, and it can be true for you, too. Let's "follow" Nehemiah as he records the reconstruction process of the gates of Jerusalem. Read Nehemiah 3:1. What is the first gate mentioned as being rebuilt?

Nehemiah begins his record of restoration at the Sheep Gate. This is no coincidence, for this gate is where sheep were formerly brought in for the temple sacrifices. It's fitting that Nehemiah starts here, **for everything begins with Jesus, the Lamb of God, who would enter Jerusalem one day and become the ultimate sacrificial Lamb on a cross to atone for the sin of all who call on His name and believe.**

2. Look up each of the following Scripture references and then note which gate each mentions.

Nehemiah 3:3 The ______________________________ Gate

The fact that the Fish Gate is after the Sheep Gate holds symbolic significance to us as Christians when we consider what Jesus told His disciples. Jesus told Peter, Andrew, James, and John—all of whom were fishermen by trade—to follow Him and become fishers of men. As followers of Christ, they had a job to do in the kingdom. We do too. Like the disciples, we're also called to be "fishers of men." The Fish Gate reminds us of this.

Nehemiah 3:6 The ______________________ Gate
(Jeshanah also means "Old")

Next, we come to the Old Gate. It's a much-needed reminder that we are wise to avoid the distractions of the world, no matter how shiny and new their appeal may be. The paths of old have been tested and found true. God is the same yesterday, today, and forever (Hebrews 13:8). And we look to the Ancient of Days to teach us and guide us.

Nehemiah 3:13 The ______________________ Gate

After the Old Gate, we come to the Valley Gate. The valley is associated with great sorrow. When Nehemiah set out to inspect the wall at night, he started at the Valley Gate (2:13), but when he later records the reconstruction efforts, he starts at the Sheep Gate (3:1). In the same way, many of our stories begin in the valley. We suffered loss and heartache, but new life begins with the Lamb of God.

3. Please read the book excerpt below and answer the questions that follow.

> **"Please accept my sincerest apologies if you were a part of my life during that unfortunate season of 'perfume' choices. . . . Poop spray that aids in covering up bathroom smells is a good thing. Poop spray that is misused as perfume, not so much." (pp. 60–61)**

Please tell me I am not the only one who has managed to do something as embarrassing as this. In a practical sense, I know we all understand the need for such "spray" in our lives. Even in biblical times they had a gate devoted to, um, such things. Read each of the following Bible verses and fill in the blank for which gate it mentions.

Nehemiah 3:14 The ______________________ Gate

You'd think the Israelites would have given this gate a more congenial name, but there's a purpose for this. Through the Dung Gate human waste and regular garbage was taken down into the valley to be burned. Spiritually speaking, the Dung Gate is where we go to remove the spiritual filth in our lives, and that happens through confession and repentance (1 John 1:9). To walk in obedience to the Lord, confession and repentance is a necessary part of every believer's life.

Nehemiah 3:15 The ______________________ Gate

The Fountain Gate is near the Pool of Siloam, where they'd go for drinking water, the kind that wells up from a nearby spring, symbolizing the Holy Spirit who dwells inside us, whose living water also springs up from within. What a tender reminder that after the deep pain of a valley and the cleansing power of confession and repentance, the Lord provides life-sustaining water through the Holy Spirit inside us.

Nehemiah 3:26 The ______________________ Gate

While the Fountain Gate offered water for drinking, the Water Gate offered water for bathing. And the Water Gate represents the Word. Imagine taking your heart in your hands and holding it under clean running water. That's what the water of the Word does for us (Ephesians 5:26). It washes us clean and renews us from the inside out.

4. Please read the book excerpt below and answer the questions that follow.

> **"Having your life turned upside down is brutally devastating, but it can help shake loose some emotionally unhealthy issues that need tending." (p. 85)**

Doing the work of building boundaries while rebuilding the areas of your life that have been devastated is nothing short of warfare. In both your heart and your soul. But we serve a God who has not left us to fight this battle on our own. Read each Bible verse below and write the name of the gate it mentions in the blank.

Nehemiah 3:28 The ______________________ Gate

Next, we come to the Horse Gate, the place near the king's stables. In times of war this is where the soldiers would come. For believers today, the Horse Gate is a symbol of the spiritual battle every believer faces. When Christ returns, he'll set up His reign for eternity. In the meantime, spiritual battles are real, and the Horse Gate immediately follows the Water Gate because the sword of the Spirit is God's Word (Ephesians 6:17). We don't need horses and physical weapons today; we battle the enemy of our souls through time in the Word and time on our knees.

Nehemiah 3:29 The ______________________ Gate

When we're feeling weary from a battle, the East Gate is the next stop around the wall of Jerusalem, and I am so grateful, because the East Gate is imbued with Ezekiel's prophetic words. In a vision Ezekiel saw the glory of the Lord depart from the temple and leave the city through the East Gate (Ezekiel 10:18–19). Then Ezekiel had another vision. He saw the glory of the Lord returning to Jerusalem one day, and when He returns, He'll come through the East Gate (Ezekiel 43:1–5). The East Gate is a symbol of hope for the future we have in Christ.

Nehemiah 3:31 The ______________________ Gate

The last gate around the wall of Jerusalem is the Inspection Gate. When a soldier returned from battle, he gave a report to the king, who'd reward him for his service. That's going to be us someday. We're going to stand before our King and give an account of our lives. We're going to tell Him about the battles we fought and the valleys we trudged through. And **we're going to fall to our knees and cry, "Thank You. It's all because of You, the Lamb of God who takes away my sin."**

5. Friend, thank you for taking this "tour" around the walls of ancient Jerusalem with me. As you can see, the restored gates told God's story of redemption. And that is our story, too, because of what Christ has done in our lives. Now, as we work to restore some of the "gates" in our own lives, I pray this inspires you to see how God is unfolding His redemptive purposes in your life. The rebuilt walls and restored gates in your life will be a part of your testimony. Because that is what Christ does. By His grace He restores us.

Let's finish our study today by reading one last passage of Scripture. Turn to Jeremiah 7:2. What does God instruct Jeremiah to do? Where is Jeremiah to carry out this command?

In a similar way, may this be our command today. To stand by the restored "gates" in our own lives and tell others of the goodness of our God.

Read Chapters 7–9

REVIEW AND READ

Use this time to go back and complete any of the reflection questions or activities from previous days this week that you weren't able to finish. Make note of any revelations you've had and reflect on any growth or personal insights you've gained.

Spend the next two days reading chapters 7, 8, and 9 in the book *Good Boundaries and Goodbyes*. Use the space below to make note of anything in the chapters that stands out to you or encourages your heart.

Schedule
WEEK 4

BEFORE GROUP GATHERING	Read chapters 7–9 in *Good Boundaries and Goodbyes* book.
GROUP GATHERING	Watch Video Session 4 Group Discussion Pages 100–108
PERSONAL STUDY DAY 1	Pages 109–114
PERSONAL STUDY DAY 2	Pages 115–119
PERSONAL STUDY DAY 3	Pages 119-122
PERSONAL STUDY DAYS 4 & 5	Read Chapters 10–11 in *Good Boundaries and Goodbyes* book and complete any unfinished personal study activities.

WEEK 4

Old Patterns, New Practices

THIS WEEK'S TRUTH TO HOLD ONTO:

"Just like sports fans show their allegiance and who they follow by wearing their team's jerseys, we are showing our allegiance to Jesus by our actions, attitude, and words."

WELCOME AND OPENING REFLECTION:

(Suggested time: 15–20 minutes)

Welcome to session 4 of *Good Boundaries and Goodbyes*.

Leader Note: Have a few people share their response to this question before starting the video:

What was your most helpful takeaway from this week's homework?

VIDEO:

(Running time: 21:30 minutes)

Leader Note: Play the video segment for session 4.

VIDEO NOTES:

Use the outline below to help you follow along with the teaching video and to take additional notes on anything that stands out to you.

When we look at the word *faith/pistis* in its original usage in the New Testament in context, often *faith* has a bigger picture of "allegiance."

If any part of us (our mind, mouth, or actions) are out of alignment, it brings into question the validity of our allegiance.

When it comes to our allegiance to Jesus, boundaries may be one of the most important things we can utilize in order for us to keep our allegiance true.

Colossians 3:1

Since, then, you have been raised with Christ, set your hearts on things above, where Christ is, seated at the right hand of God.

Ephesians 2:6

And God raised us up with Christ and seated us with him in the heavenly realms in Christ Jesus, . . .

This is so significant because this indicates we have a place of belonging and authority that is given to us by Jesus.

Boundaries aren't just so that we can stay in a good mood and be nice to others; it's so we can actually keep the best of who Christ has called us to be intact—keeping our thoughts and our heart motives in line with biblical wisdom and instruction.

We will make mistakes . . . but putting off the old self means we will no longer make these behaviors so normal that they become practices or ongoing patterns of behavior.

When we say the peace of Christ rules in our heart, what we're really saying is we are willingly submitting ourselves to the ways of Jesus.

Colossians 3:10

. . . and have put on the new self, which is being renewed in knowledge in the image of its Creator.

Paul tells us to put on our victory clothes given to us by Jesus that gives the world evidence of our faithful allegiance to Jesus.

The boundaries we put in place are actually safeguards that help align our actions, our attitude, and our words with God's instructions, and keeps our allegiance to victorious King Jesus intact and evident for others to witness.

One of our whole goals of putting boundaries on ourselves and in relationships is to prevent us from getting to that worn down, worn out place from unhealthy relationships that our pattern starts to be harshness instead of gentleness, chaos instead of peace, ungratefulness or grumpiness instead of gratitude.

Group DISCUSSION

(Suggested Time: 40–45 Minutes)

Leader Note: We have suggested questions to start with, but feel free to pick any of the additional questions as well. Consider the timeframe of your group and know the ultimate goal is meaningful discussion.

SUGGESTED QUESTIONS . . .

1. As you consider some of the allegiances in your own life, what might others say your allegiances are based on your attitudes, actions, and words? Share your responses with your group.

2. In what ways is your faith—your allegiance to Jesus—evident in your words and actions? In what ways would you like to grow so that your faith and allegiance to Jesus is more evident to others?

3. Read Colossians 3:1. If members of your group have different Bible translations, have each person share Colossians 3:1 from their Bible's version. Then write out this verse in the space below with your own Bible's translation.

4. Read Romans 6:4; Colossians 2:12; and Ephesians 2:6. What does it mean that you and I have been "raised with Christ"? How does this truth convey the idea that Jesus has given us a place of belonging and authority?

5. What practical imagery is being used in Colossians 3:9 and Colossians 3:10? Now consider the lists provided in Colossians 3:5–9 and Colossians 3:10–14. What, if anything, stands out to you as something you need to "put off" or something you need to "put on"? Write down what you sense God telling you. Then share with your group.

ADDITIONAL QUESTIONS . . .

6. According to Colossians 3:15, what are we supposed to let rule in our hearts?

7. Sometimes when we are experiencing turmoil in a relationship, we can feel paralyzed if the other person isn't willing or capable of working with us to get to a better place. Read Romans 12:18 and fill in the blanks below. (The following passage is taken from the NIV.)

   "If it is ______________________________, as far as it depends on ________, live at ________________ with ______________________."

   Notice how Paul doesn't say, "It depends on you to be at peace with everyone," as if it's all up to you to keep the peace. Nope. Paul prefaces his command with the key words, "If it is possible," because Paul knows that perfect harmony with everybody isn't always possible in this broken world. We are not responsible for keeping the peace at all costs. We are only responsible for ourselves, for our own words and actions. And good boundaries help us do just that. How does knowing this release you from the unrealistic expectation that you are somehow supposed to live peaceably with all people at all times?

8. When you are facing an extremely difficult situation, the Bible doesn't promise an easy exit or a way to escape the pain. But it does tell us that every situation is under God's sovereign hand. We can't always see *how* God is moving in a situation, but we can trust that God *is* moving. This is how we can have peace in the midst of very trying circumstances. Have a different member of your group look up and read aloud one of the following verses. Then answer the following questions together.

   Read 2 Thessalonians 3:16. Who gives us peace? And how often?

Read Isaiah 9:6. In regard to peace, what is one of Jesus's official titles?

Read Philippians 4:4–7. What does peace do to our hearts?

Read Isaiah 26:3. What happens when we place our trust in God?

CLOSING: (Suggested time: 5 minutes)

Leader Note: End your session by reading the "Between-Sessions Personal Studies" instructions to the group and making sure there are no questions pertaining to the homework. Then take a few minutes to pray over your group, either reading the provided prayer aloud over them or praying your own prayer.

BETWEEN-SESSIONS PERSONAL STUDIES . . .

Every week in the *Good Boundaries and Goodbyes Study Guide* includes five days of personal study to help you make meaningful connections between your life and what you're learning each week. This week, you'll work with the material in chapters 7–9 of the book *Good Boundaries and Goodbyes.* You'll also have time to read chapters 10–11 of the book in preparation for our next session together.

PRAYER

Lord, thank You that we can come to You, and by Your grace we can "put off" our old self and we can "put on" our new self, for we are a new creation in You. In You all things are made new. When we make mistakes and fail to live up to Your commands, we ask for Your forgiveness, and we ask that You strengthen us so we may walk in a manner worthy of the faith we profess in You, for we want our words and our actions to be a testimony of where our true allegiance lies. We thank You for the peace You give, for You are the Prince of Peace. When certain moments in our day threaten to unravel our peace, help us to look to You as the firm foundation on which we stand. We love You, Lord. In Jesus' name, amen.

Personal STUDY

DAY 1

Read Chapter 7

One of the greatest benefits to having good boundaries in our lives is that good boundaries help us to know where we end and another person begins. On the surface, that statement may sound too elementary, but healthy relationships are healthy in large part because one person isn't constantly trying to change the other person or manage their opinions. We can be secure in our own identity and operate as a whole person, responsible for our own actions. **Healthy people understand where their responsibilities end and the other person's responsibilities begin.**

Good boundaries, then, can functionally serve as markers reminding us that we can't be all things to all people . . . we have limitations. And when we have a healthy respect for our capacities and limits, we are more likely to communicate those to others and much less likely to extend ourselves beyond what is reasonable and then become a tired, frustrated mess.

In our personal study time this week we will explore some ways that good boundaries help us preserve the best of who we are.

In Day 1, we will answer the question, "Who am I?"

In Day 2, we will answer the question, "What makes me whole?"

In Day 3, we will answer the question, "Can I really break free from people pleasing?"

First, be sure to read chapter 7 in the book *Good Boundaries and Goodbyes*, then go ahead jump into today's lesson!

1. Please read the book excerpt below and answer the questions that follow.

> **"The [wrong or misguided] mindset I mentioned at the beginning of this chapter is this: people's opinions define who we are. If we live with this mindset, we will be desperate to try and control people's perceptions of us. We will spend our lives managing opinions to always be favorable toward us so we can feel good about ourselves." (p. 101)**

   Honestly, when I lived this way, it was exhausting. It's just not possible to control everyone else's opinions all the time. So, the more I tried, the more tired I became. Can you relate to letting other people's opinions define who you are? Why is this an exercise in futility?

2. Breaking free from this mindset—of always needing other people to think well of me—has been a pivotal keystone of growth in my life. Which is why I am so passionate about helping friends like you break free from this mindset, too! Open your Bible and read Galatians 1:10. Whose approval truly matters?

3. Please read the book excerpt below and answer the questions that follow.

> **"I think this hits at the core fear around setting boundaries: If I set a boundary, someone will no longer see me as I want them to see me. They will no longer know me as I want them to know me. They will no longer believe the best about me, and there's something inside of me that really wants them to believe the best about me." (p. 102)**

This right here is one of the biggest hurdles to implementing good boundaries in our lives. Fear. Especially the fear of being misunderstood. Think of a time when you've been misunderstood by someone close to you, or someone you hoped would like you. What happened? How did the misunderstanding make you feel? How have situations like that supported your avoidance of establishing good boundaries out of fear of being misunderstood again?

4. Let's look at a woman in the Bible who was seriously misunderstood—and by a priest no less! Read 1 Samuel 1:1–14. How was Hannah misunderstood by the priest Eli?

5. How can we be sure that God never misunderstands us? Read Jeremiah 17:10 and 1 Samuel 16:7. What can God always see?

6. Please read the book excerpt below and answer the questions that follow.

> **"Somewhere in all the looking around at others for validation, we've stopped looking up. If we are living honest lives that honor God, we must not forget that people not being 'good' with us does not mean we aren't living right before God." (p. 108)**

God sees our hearts. He knows our honest intentions and truest motivations. So, if we are living right before God and we are moving through our days with a clear conscience, then we can stand firmly, knowing that God knows everything. He knows the facts about every situation. And He knows our hearts. God sees and God knows. And the only person whose approval we truly need, is God's. When these truths are firmly planted in our souls, we don't have to look around at others for validation. Read Hebrews 12:2; Proverbs 4:25–27; and Deuteronomy 5:32. Where do these verses tell us to keep our eyes fixed?

How do you do this on a daily basis? What distracts you or hinders you from keeping your eyes fixed on Jesus?

7. Please read the book excerpt below and answer the question that follows.

> **"While checking ourselves is healthy, questioning our identity is not. Checking ourselves means looking at a current attitude or behavior to see if it is in line with God's instructions and wisdom. Questioning our identity is doubting who we are because we have given too much power to other people by letting their opinions define us." (p. 108)**

To have healthy boundaries, we must settle this question in our hearts: *Who am I?* To firmly answer this question, read John 1:12; 1 Corinthians 12:27; 2 Corinthians 5:17; and Psalm 139:13–16. Who does the Bible say you are?

8. Please read the book excerpt below and answer the questions that follow.

> **"We want to let God's Word become the words of truth for our identity. When God is the source of our identity, we are much less prone to others feeding our insecurity." (p. 114)**

Choose one of the verses from question 7 and make it your anthem. You are a child of God. You are a new creation in Christ. You are a member in Christ's family, a part of His body. And you were seen and known even in your mother's womb. This means God has always known you. And He has always chosen you. God is the reason we can go from being misunderstood to known, accepted, chosen, and loved. Finish your personal study time today by writing out a prayer, thanking God for the identity He has given you as His precious daughter.

Read Chapter 8

Today we're going to explore chapter 8 of the book *Good Boundaries and Goodbyes*. If you haven't already read chapter 8, please do so now.

1. Please read the book excerpt below and answer the questions that follow.

> **"Sometimes the worst kind of anger and bitterness happens when you feel forced to smile on the outside while you are screaming on the inside. I've been that woman. Sometimes losing my temper because I'd let things go so long, I just couldn't hold back my frustration any longer. Or, sometimes biting my tongue so long that I lost the desire to ever speak to that person again. I'm not proud of either of these extremes. And neither of these reactions match who I really am as a person. . . . I knew I needed boundaries, so why was I letting other people's commentary rattle my identity?" (pp. 121–122)**

Can you relate to either of these extremes? Holding in your frustration so long that you eventually exploded in anger? Or, holding your tongue so long that you lost the desire even to speak to that person again? What emotions were you feeling when that happened?

2. God-informed boundaries hold us together when life around us is falling apart. They help us avoid the extremes of losing our temper or going completely silent while suffering deeply inside. Let's look at a woman in the Bible who had a moment where she completely lost it, and in her anger and bitterness, she treated someone else badly.

   Read Genesis 16:1–6. What happened between Sarai and Hagar? What did Hagar do after Sarai treated her so badly?

3. My friend, let's pause for a minute and discuss the tragic nature of an occurrence in biblical times: some men married more than one wife. Please know that this was never God's design for marriage (Genesis 2:24). The stories of polygamy in the Bible are *describing* what happened in the lives of broken people living in a broken world, and these stories are not in any way *prescribing* how people ought to live. In so many stories in the Bible where this occurs, we see devastating heartbreak for everyone involved. This is because God's boundaries for marriage had been tragically violated.

   For Sarai, she was so desperate to have a family she initiated a disastrous plan. But once Hagar became pregnant, the reality of it all set in and Sarai couldn't contain the years of anguish she had experienced in her barrenness. Now everyone would know that it was Sarai's body that wasn't working properly and not Abraham's. And poor Hagar was a slave without any personal agency of her own. This whole situation was a horrible mess for everyone. That's what happens when God's boundaries for healthy living and healthy marriages are violated. Pain is everywhere.

   Please read the book excerpt below and answer the questions that follow.

   > **"Certainly drawing boundaries in a marriage where infidelity and other traumatic issues are happening apply to some of us but not all of us. Regardless, we all must not just draw appropriate boundaries but also guard our true identity." (p. 126)**

Every relationship—whether it's between a husband and a wife, or between two siblings or two friends or two neighbors, or between an employer and an employee—needs good boundaries. They help us to avoid extreme reactions, and they hold together who we really are in the face of adversity. What does this look like in practical everyday terms? Read Micah 6:8 and fill in the blanks below. (The following passage is taken from the NIV.)

"He has shown you, O mortal, what is ________. And what does the LORD ____________ of you? To act _________ and to love ____________ and to walk ____________ with your God."

4. In chapter 8 you read the definition of wholeness as being when orthodoxy, orthopathy, and orthopraxy are in alignment with who God intends for us to be. These are some big words, so let's unpack them a little more here.

   Orthodoxy involves correct doctrine. It's what we ____________________________.

   Orthopathy involves correct emotions. It's what we ___________________________.

   Orthopraxy involves correct living. It's what we _____________________________.

   It's amazing to think that God cares about all three of these deeply personal areas in our lives. What we know. What we feel. What we do. Now, let's connect this definition of wholeness with God's commands in Micah 6:8. Draw a line connecting each part of wholeness to God's commands in Micah 6:8.

Act justly.	**Orthopathy:** Feeling genuine compassion.
Love mercy.	**Orthopraxy:** Living rightly.
Walk humbly.	**Orthodoxy:** Knowing what is good and true.

   And when all three of these areas are in alignment with God's truths, we can walk through our days with a steady confidence.

5. Please read the book excerpt below and answer the questions that follow.

> **"[B]eing whole has a big impact on not only our health but on the quality of the relationships we are drawn to. Whole people tend to gravitate toward whole people. Fractured people tend to attract other fractured people." (p. 129)**

While many broken people were drawn to Jesus, it was their desire for wholeness that drew them to Him. And those who did not desire genuine wholeness from the inside out were repelled by Jesus. Read Isaiah 53:2–5; Luke 2:52; 4:22; Matthew 7:28–29; John 7:18. Make a list below of Jesus's attributes that drew people to Him.

6. Jesus is the perfect picture of wholeness in any person who ever walked this earth. So, when people are committed to becoming more like Christ, then they are committed to growing in wholeness. Read Galatians 3:26–29; Ephesians 5:1–2; and 1 Corinthians 6:19–20. How does this passage speak to our identity and then give clear commands for daily living? Why is it so important that the matter of our identity be settled before we can wholly live out God's commands?

7. Finish today's personal study time in prayer, asking God to show you one area where you need to grow in wholeness. Maybe it's in orthodoxy. Or maybe it's in orthopathy or orthopraxy? Or maybe you want to work on all three of these things to be better aligned—so what you think, feel, and do are all consistently honoring God. Write down what you want to focus on the most right now and then consider some practical ways you might live this out in the coming days.

Read Chapter 9

Today we're going to examine chapter 9 of the book *Good Boundaries and Goodbyes*. If you haven't read chapter 9 yet, you'll want to do that now.

1. Please read the book excerpt below and answer the questions that follow.

> **"[Do] you hear the difference there between 'I want to be' and 'I must be'? *I want to be* is driven by a desire. *I must be* is driven by a demand. And when our desires shift into becoming demands, we run the risk of getting caught in the most serious form of people pleasing." (p. 144)**

Some desires are good. Sometimes they're even placed in our hearts by God. But when desires morph into demands, we drift into dangerous territory. Read the story in Judges 16:4–21. What did Delilah repeatedly ask of Samson? Were her requests more of a desire or a demand? See Judges 16:16.

2. Healthy desires stem from a will to get your needs met while not compromising the good of the other person; whereas, demands stem from a will of self-gain. And when we give in to the demands of others, it's oftentimes due to a fear that our own needs will go unmet if we don't do what they want. When have you given in to the demands of someone and later regretted it? What was your underlying motivation for giving in? (See the list of needs on pages 145–146.)

3. Please read the book excerpt below and answer the questions that follow.

> **"People pleasing isn't just about keeping others happy. It's about getting from them what we think we must have in order to feel okay in the world. . . . The less we get what we feel we need from someone, the more we are tempted to react in extremes. Either we drain ourselves through all manner of people pleasing, or we eventually give up and walk away." (p. 146)**

It's not wrong to have needs and desires. And it's not wrong for other people to have needs and desires. But it is unhealthy to extend ourselves beyond our human, finite limits in an effort either to meet the demands of the other person or to gain for ourselves whatever it is we think we need. When we do this, our desires have shifted into demands, and even if we get what we think we need, it is short-lived. Before long, we'll be back repeating the same unhealthy patterns. So, is it possible to break free from the unhealthy cycle of people pleasing? Yes! Read Psalm 121:1–2 and Philippians 4:19. Where does our help come from? Who is the Provider and Sustainer of our most genuine needs?

4. Let's look at an example in Scripture of when the people failed to trust God as their Provider. Read Exodus 16:11–30. Why were God's people supposed to collect twice as much manna on the sixth day of each week?

   If it wasn't the Sabbath, what would happen if they tried to hoard some until the following morning?

   When they stored extra food for the following day, and it wasn't the Sabbath, what did this signify in their hearts?

5. In what ways do you struggle to trust God to provide for your physical and/or emotional needs?

6. Please read the book excerpt below and answer the questions that follow.

> **"So, what do we do if we are caught in the trap of this type of people-pleasing agenda? It starts with managing our own thought life." (p. 150)**

Some of us fear there will be a devastating gap between what we think we need and what God will actually provide. It can lead us to try and get from people what we are unsure God will provide. But good boundaries help to reign in this temptation, and it begins when we place boundaries around our thought life. We must make the conscious choice to lead our thoughts toward what pleases God. Read Romans 8:5–6; 12:2; 2 Corinthians 10:5; Philippians 4:8–9. In the space below, summarize the core thought around these verses.

7. Let's conclude today's personal study time by contemplating the many ways God has shown Himself faithful in providing for your needs. Whether you have walked with God a long time or you're fairly new in this faith journey, write down some of the ways God has provided for you. Then thank Him for these provisions and ask Him to help you grow in your trust in Him as your Provider. For when you can trust that God will meet your truest needs, then you can begin to break free from the unhealthy patterns of people pleasing.

Read Chapters 10–11

REVIEW AND READ

Use this time to go back and complete any of the reflection questions or activities from previous days this week that you weren't able to finish. Make note of any revelations you've had and reflect on any growth or personal insights you've gained.

Spend the next two days reading chapters 10 and 11 in the book *Good Boundaries and Goodbyes*. Use the space below to make note of anything in the chapters that stands out to you or encourages your heart.

Schedule
WEEK 5

BEFORE GROUP GATHERING	Read chapters 10–11 in *Good Boundaries and Goodbyes* book.
GROUP GATHERING	Watch Video Session 5 Group Discussion Pages 126–134
PERSONAL STUDY DAY 1	Pages 135–139
PERSONAL STUDY DAY 2	Pages 140–144
PERSONAL STUDY DAY 3	Pages 145–149
PERSONAL STUDY DAYS 4 & 5	Read Chapter 12 and the Conclusion in *Good Boundaries and Goodbyes* book and complete any unfinished personal study activities.

WEEK 5

People in the Bible Who Had to **Say Hard Goodbyes**

THIS WEEK'S TRUTH TO HOLD ONTO:

"We need to keep our hearts willing to still obey God in the midst of our separations and goodbyes."

WELCOME AND OPENING REFLECTION:

(Suggested time: 15–20 minutes)

Welcome to session 5 of *Good Boundaries and Goodbyes.*

Leader Note: Have a few people share their response to this question before starting the video:

What was your most helpful takeaway from this week's homework?

VIDEO:

(Running time: 30:30 minutes)

Leader Note: Play the video segment for session 5.

VIDEO NOTES:

Use the outline below to help you follow along with the teaching video and to take additional notes on anything that stands out to you.

At some point in all of our lives, we will have to face some goodbyes. And many times those goodbyes are hard, excruciating, heartbreaking seasons.

There are usually three scenarios for goodbyes:

- Sometimes people are sent away.
- Sometimes people walk away.
- Sometimes there is a parting of ways.

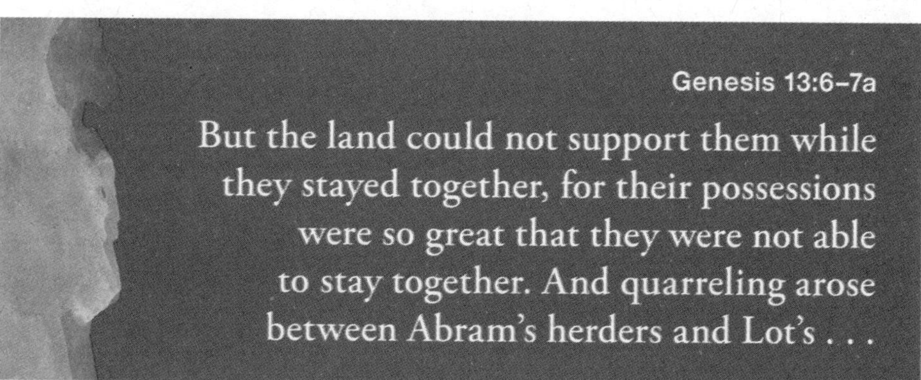

Abraham is proactive. . . . He sees the beginnings of a type of dysfunction that would lead to eventual tragic disunity, so he makes the decision that it would be better for them to separate.

Abraham didn't allow his heart to be hardened by it.

In Genesis, whenever people move "east," it has a negative context as it relates to moving away from God or into danger.

Abraham doesn't chase him down and try to force him to make another choice. But as we see years later, Abraham didn't carry bitterness and simmering resentments over the disappointment of Lot's choice.

Abraham's heart was always in a posture of compassion (not enabling) toward Lot.

Acts 15:39–40

[Paul and Barnabas] had such a sharp disagreement that they parted company. Barnabas took Mark and sailed for Cyprus, but Paul chose Silas and left, commended by the believers to the grace of the Lord.

Verse 39 reads that this was a "sharp disagreement." These words are important, and they mean that there was an extremely charged emotional response from both sides.

Both [Paul and Barnabas] are commended. They both have reasons for the parting of ways that make sense, and they both act out of personal conviction and the boundaries they needed to establish.

As a result, their goodbye actually allowed something good; it allowed the gospel to spread in two different directions and that went even further than if they had stayed together.

This is the beauty of good boundaries and goodbyes. When done appropriately, they give relationships the space necessary to possibly heal and get better over time. This isn't always possible, but it is in some cases where boundaries and goodbyes help prevent the total destruction of a relationship.

GOOD WORDS TO REMEMBER:

Jesus had relational challenges with Peter and Judas—people who were very close to Him. – Dr. Joel Muddamalle

Our words frame our reality. – Jim Cress

The more they spin, the further they're getting away from repentance. – Jim Cress

Notice how the enemy uses verses out of context in the temptation scene with Jesus to try and create a disorientation. – Dr. Joel Muddamalle

If there is an active addiction and that person is not healthy . . . say, "I will not be in a relationship with someone in an active addiction . . . who will not go get that addiction treated." – Jim Cress

To get free access to a bonus session where we continue this conversation with Lysa, Jim and Joel go to PROVERBS31.ORG/BOUNDARIES-EXTRAS

Group DISCUSSION

(Suggested Time: 40–45 Minutes)

Leader Note: We have suggested questions to start with, but feel free to pick any of the additional questions as well. Consider the timeframe of your group and know the ultimate goal is meaningful discussion.

SUGGESTED QUESTIONS . . .

1. Have you ever experienced teaching within the church or by a mature believer on necessary endings or appropriate goodbyes? If so, what did you learn? If not, why do you think this topic isn't talked about very much?

2. Consider the three scenarios for goodbyes: 1) Sometimes people are sent away. 2) Sometimes people walk away. 3) Sometimes there is a mutual parting of ways. Have you experienced a goodbye that falls into one of these three scenarios? How is it helpful to know there is actually biblical precedent for each of the three scenarios?

3. There will be seasons in our lives when we are called to stay, to plant roots, and to work hard for the preservation of what is growing. Read Jeremiah 42:1–10. Through the prophet Jeremiah, what did God command His people to do?

4. There will also be seasons in our lives when we are called to uproot and move far away, or to separate from all that is familiar. Read Genesis 12:1. What did God call Abraham and his entire household to do?

5. What does Ecclesiastes 3:1–2 tell us?

6. Spend some time in your group, sharing about a season in your life when you were called to stay. Then share about a season in your life when you were called to go. How did God show Himself faithful in each of those seasons?

ADDITIONAL QUESTIONS . . .

7. While Abraham's situation is unique, there are principles here for us to glean. Read Genesis 12:2–5 and Hebrews 11:6, 8. We discussed earlier how faith (the Greek word *pistis*) is akin to showing our allegiance. How did Abraham show his allegiance to this unseen God? (Remember, in Abraham's world, most "gods" were man-made idols that one could see with their eyes.) What was Abraham "losing" by leaving? What was he gaining?

8. Leaving is hard. Saying goodbye to loved ones is hard. But sometimes it is the very thing God calls us to do. Not as a sort of punishment. But because God has plans beyond anything we can see or imagine. Even in those really hard seasons, when our suffering has been deep and long, there are reasons beyond what we can see and know in the here and now. What truth does Paul remind us of in Romans 8:28 and Ephesians 3:20–21?

9. Is there a goodbye you are considering in your life right now? What biblical wisdom is helping you navigate this decision? Of the three scenarios for parting we discussed, which does your potential goodbye fall within? If you feel comfortable, perhaps share with your group what you are currently facing and ask for prayer.

CLOSING: (Suggested time: 5 minutes)

Leader Note: End your session by reading the "Between-Sessions Personal Studies" instructions to the group and making sure there are no questions pertaining to the homework. Then take a few minutes to pray over your group, either reading the provided prayer aloud over them or praying your own prayer.

BETWEEN-SESSIONS PERSONAL STUDIES . . .

Every week in the *Good Boundaries and Goodbyes Study Guide* includes five days of personal study to help you make meaningful connections between your life and what you're learning each week. This week, you'll work with the material in chapters 10–11 of the book *Good Boundaries and Goodbyes*. You'll also have time to read chapter 12 and the conclusion of the book in preparation for our next session together.

PRAYER

Lord, when we are facing hard decisions—like whether to stay or go—we know we can come to You with our questions and struggles. We thank You for providing us with wisdom and guidance through Your Word, Your Spirit, and through godly counsel. Help us not to rush into any decision but to wait on You for direction. Help us to linger in Your presence until Your peace has so filled us that we are then confident with the choice we have before us. We place every decision we face into Your capable hands. We look to You first in everything we do. Because we trust You, knowing You have only the best intentions toward us as Your children. We love You and praise You, Lord. In Jesus' name, amen.

Personal STUDY

DAY 1

Read Chapter 10

In both this week's video teaching and in the reading, we are discussing the joyful reality that sometimes our good boundaries will lead to the ministry of reconciliation that we have hoped and prayed and worked so very hard for.

Other times, however, our good boundaries will lead us to say a necessary goodbye. And when it becomes necessary and right to say goodbye, we can do this with grace and goodwill as we follow the Bible's guidance and teaching on this topic.

For our personal study time this week, we will examine what it looks like to live in wholeness on the other side of a goodbye.

In Day 1, we'll discuss how to make peace with the memories.

In Day 2, we'll explore how to yield to the renovation process.

In Day 3, we'll talk about how to accept the outcomes we didn't want.

If you haven't had a chance yet to read chapter 10, you'll want to do that now.

1. In the teaching video and in Chapter 10, we saw three biblical examples of three different scenarios when a goodbye became necessary.

   - Abraham and Lot

   - Paul and Barnabas

   - Jesus and the Rich Young Ruler

We learned that some goodbyes are for a season while others are forever. But in every goodbye, we can be God-honoring in how we move through the goodbye. Read Psalm 1:1–3 and Colossians 3:17. How can these verses pertain to saying good goodbyes as well?

2. Please read the book excerpt below and answer the question that follows.

> **"So, yeah, you and I are so much more alike than what we'd ever know if we were just passing each other in the bread aisle at the grocery on a random Wednesday morning. We'd both look pretty normal, moving along with the practical details our lives require. And yet somewhere between deciding to go with the whole wheat or skip the bread altogether this week, a memory from the past flashes across your mind and, as you sigh, invisible grief spills out with your exhaled breath." (p. 160)**

Without warning, our grief can bubble up at the most unexpected times. Like in the bread aisle at the grocery store. Has grief ever flooded over you at unexpected times or places? In the space below, write down what triggered your grief unexpectedly.

3. Memories. They're both our greatest treasures and our deepest sorrows. And sometimes it can be hard to hold them both within the same heart. Even in some church contexts, there can be a subtle pressure to act like we have everything together when just beneath the surface we're hurting and we don't know how to express it. Thankfully, God welcomes and understands the lament of his children. Read Psalms 6:3; 38:9–10; 130:1–2. If you were to write a one- or two-sentence lament as a prayer to God, what would you write?

4. Please read the book excerpt below and answer the questions that follow.

> **"Maybe it is possible to end a relationship, being honest about what wasn't healthy, and still celebrate what was good." (p. 161)**

Certainly, there are some situations that are so horrific it's an injustice to try to conjure up something "good" about it. Our purpose here is not to wrap a tidy bow around every memory we have. At the same time, there are some goodbyes that, while necessary in the end, can still hold something beautiful, especially in an earlier time when things were healthier. An element of parting with grace and wisdom is being able to decipher the good from the not-so-good. To recognize with clarity which parts were unhealthy while appreciating the parts that, for a time, were indeed good. Can you think of a situation that bore a complicated mixture of both good and not-so-good memories? Which is easier for you? Remembering only the good? Focusing solely on the bad? Or, embracing a mixture of both?

5. The command to remember is prevalent throughout much of the Bible. Most of the time it's in the context of remembering the good things God has done. His deliverance. His redemption. His provision. And so much more. Read Joshua 4:1–7. What purpose did the stones serve?

6. One of the ways we can begin to experience healing from painful memories is to focus on remembering God's goodness, God's presence, and God's faithfulness. Begin writing a list of the ways you remember God coming through for you in a difficult season. Or, maybe a time when God's presence was keenly felt in a time of great sorrow. Or, a time when God showed Himself faithful. Sometimes these memory muscles need strengthening. So, as you begin this list, come back to it later to add additional remembrances as you think of more. If at first it seems hard to think of anything, ask God to reveal to you the ways He has truly been an ever-present help.

7. Please read the book excerpt below and answer the questions that follow.

> **"I don't want to be a pit dweller. I want to walk in the light. I want to delight in the truth. And I want my heart, mind, and words to reflect my devotion to God. I will not bow down to someone's mistreatment, but I also will not rise up with such angst and anger that I violate God's truth in the way I exit. I'd like a little more 'God be with you' in my goodbyes." (p. 167)**

What part of a goodbye you've experienced has tempted you to be a pit dweller? What are some of the ways you've personally walked in the light, delighted in the truth, and kept your devotion to God even when someone else broke your heart by walking away?

8. Let's close today's personal study time with the exercise I mentioned at the end of chapter 10. Close your eyes and picture Jesus' hands. One by one, begin placing each painful memory into His strong and capable hands. As you place each sorrowful memory there, whisper "God be with you." And let Christ's peace wash over you.

Read Chapter 11

Today we're going to reflect on chapter 11 of the book *Good Boundaries and Goodbyes*. If you haven't read chapter 11 yet, please do so before you begin.

1. Please read the book excerpt below and answer the questions that follow.

> **"A renovation is a temporary setback that is actually a setup for something even more beautiful. There's a plan and when you stay true to the plan, you know what's being torn apart is for the purpose of being put back together better and stronger than before." (p. 177)**

In many ways, the renovations being done to my home paralleled the renovations that were happening in my life. It wasn't easy. Sometimes it felt like chaos and debris were all around me. But I knew that if I stuck to the boundaries I had worked so hard to establish, then the beauty that was currently under construction would eventually become evident. Have you ever lived in a house that was undergoing a major renovation or reconstruction? Or, have you ever watched one of those shows that depicts a home getting stripped down to the studs and then rebuilt? Why is it necessary to strip away so much of the old before rebuilding with the new?

2. How is this renovation process also displayed in our lives sometimes? Can you think of a time when you have personally experienced a "stripping away" before "rebuilding the new"?

3. In more ways than one, we serve a God who specializes in creating beauty from ashes. Read Isaiah 61:3 and Luke 4:14–21. How does the passage in Isaiah point forward to Christ? And how does the passage in Luke become the fulfillment of the passage in Isaiah?

4. Read Ephesians 2:10 and fill in the blanks below. (The following passage is taken from the NIV.)

   "For we are God's ______________________, created in Christ Jesus to do good works, which God prepared in advance for us to do."

   Some translations say *handiwork*. Some say *workmanship*. Some say *masterpiece*. The Greek word being used here is *poiema* and it has to do with God actively bringing into existence creation and new creation. This is where we get today's English word *poem*. Think about that. Poems are created and brought about by an author for a specific purpose. You are God's poem. And everything you have been through, or may be currently going through, God can use to create something beautiful from the ashes in your life.

5. Please read the book excerpt below and answer the questions that follow.

> **"When a relationship shifts from being difficult to being destructive, it's the right time to consider a goodbye." (p. 179)**

This was key for me. Recognizing the difference between a difficult relationship and a destructive relationship. With the latter being the indicator that a goodbye is needed. Only then can the renovation process begin. Otherwise, I am still caught in the cycle of chaos. Is there a relationship in your life that has moved from difficult to destructive? What are some of the distinctive signs? And who can be a safe person for you to process this with?

6. Please read the book excerpt below and answer the questions that follow.

> **"Now, this doesn't mean we can't love someone who is in active sin. But it does mean we don't participate in what they choose to do. And we don't allow their choices to harm us and start drawing our heart into places of compromise, devastation, or deception. Again, we all need grace when we mess up. But we also need the awareness that there is a difference between an occasional slip in behavior and an ongoing pattern of behavior." (pp. 182–183)**

How can we know if someone we are in a relationship with is making occasional errors in judgment or is embracing an on-going pattern of wrong behavior? Read David's confession in Psalm 51. What is David's plea?

After David's personal moral failure, he confessed his sin and repented. To repent means to change or to turn from one's sin. David didn't just say he was sorry and then continue his life of sin. No, David sought God with his whole heart for forgiveness. Being in a right relationship with God was of utmost importance to him. And that is the difference.

7. True heart renovation begins with repentance and leads to genuine, sustained change. That doesn't mean we'll never mess up or be in need of God's grace again, but it does mean that we are consistently and intentionally living out the good standing we have with God because of the work of Jesus on the cross. Read Psalm 27:4, which was also written by David. How does this psalm depict a heart that continuously longs for God? How can you make this your heart's cry, too?

8. Please read the book excerpt below and answer the questions that follow.

> **"I don't mind living through hard renovations because I always have a vision for something better that will surely come from all the hardship. Just like I could withstand the chaos of a renovation and still love this old house through it all, I can do that with people too." (p. 177)**

Bring today's personal study time to a close by reflecting on an area in your life that may be currently "under renovation" or needs to be "under renovation." Do you have a vision for what it will be like on the other side of that renovation? How can this vision help you press on through the hardships and chaos right now?

Without this vision of the beauty that is just waiting to unfold, it will be hard to see the renovation through to the other side. In the space below, write a few words that describe your vision for what life will be like on the other side of this renovation. And if you are hard-pressed for words, write a prayer asking God to show you a vision of what He is currently working out in your life.

DAY 3

My counselor, Jim Cress, has said to me time and again, "Mental health is a commitment to reality at all costs." I like the part about "a commitment to reality." It's the part about "at all costs" that gives me pause. If something is going to cost us, it means a loss to us of some kind. And nobody enjoys loss.

But if we are going to be serious about making peace with our memories and yielding to the process of renovation, then we must also be serious about accepting our reality. This is, of course, much easier said than done. But **with the power of God's Spirit inside us and God's Word to guide us and godly counsel to stand beside us, we can do this.** We can accept the changes that must be made for the sake of our health and the health of those around us.

Today we will continue our personal study time with what we learned in chapter 11.

1. The theme for today's study is acceptance of reality—no matter the cost. Let's look at some examples in the Bible and consider the circumstances people either rejected or accepted.

    - Read 1 Chronicles 17:1–2. What did King David desire to do? Was this a good desire?

    - Read 1 Chronicles 22:6–8. Did God grant King David's desire? Why or why not?

    - Read 1 Chronicles 22:9–16. How is it evident that King David accepted the reality that he would not be the one to build the temple for God?

- Let's look at one more example. Read Luke 1:26–37. What new reality did Mary face with the angel's news? How was this both "good news" and "bad news" for Mary personally?

- Now read Luke 1:38. What was Mary's response to her new reality?

2. What we see in both King David's life and Mary's life is that their acceptance of reality came at a cost to them personally. King David would not be the one to build the temple for God even though it was a great desire of his to do so. And Mary would likely face the scorn and ridicule of others, due to her "unwed pregnancy," for much of her life. But both accepted their realities because they trusted that God was at work in ways that were bigger than either of them. If you were to give words to your reality right now, what would you say? Use the space below to describe your current reality.

3. In many ways, giving words to your reality is a huge part of accepting your reality. Now, I want you to do one more thing. Ask yourself: *Am I at peace with my current reality? Why or why not?* Write your response below.

4. Please read the book excerpt below and answer the question that follows.

> **"If peace isn't possible in the current circumstances in a relationship, then we must strive to find peace with that person by changing the circumstances or changing the relationship." (pp. 188–189)**

What part of this statement resonates most with you?

5. Please read the book excerpt below and answer the question that follows.

> **"A big part of setting boundaries in even the best of circumstances is accepting the reality that when you know a change needs to happen, you need to move toward making it happen. You don't have to make all the changes at once. And you don't have to start with the biggest change. But whatever reality is telling you, and however the Lord is leading you, move toward that." (p. 178)**

What changes, if any, are you sensing the Lord leading you toward?

6. Let's look at one more example from Scripture of someone accepting their extremely hard reality, even at tremendous personal cost. Read Matthew 26:36–39. What is the prayer Jesus prayed? What statement indicates that Jesus fully accepted the reality He was facing?

7. Read Hebrews 12:2. Why did Jesus accept the horrific reality of the cross? What exactly was the "joy" that was set before Him?

8. You, my friend, are God's joy. Jesus, the King of the universe, was willing to endure the crucifixion of His own body so He could be the instrument of spiritual renovation to your soul. As you finish today's personal study time and contemplate what changes, if any, the Lord may be leading you toward, remember the goal of good boundaries—to hold together the best of who God created you to be—and also remember the goal of

any renovation—to behold the beauty waiting to unfold in you. Write a prayer of thanks, knowing that God is working in ways that you may not be able to fully see yet, but you trust that His intentions toward you are good.

Read Chapter 12 and the Conclusion

REVIEW AND READ

Use this time to go back and complete any of the reflection questions or activities from previous days this week that you weren't able to finish. Make note of any revelations you've had and reflect on any growth or personal insights you've gained.

Spend the next two days reading chapter 12 and the conclusion in the book *Good Boundaries and Goodbyes*. Use the space below to make note of anything in the chapters that stands out to you or encourages your heart.

Schedule
WEEK 6

BEFORE GROUP GATHERING	Read chapter 12 and the conclusion in *Good Boundaries and Goodbyes* book
GROUP GATHERING	Watch Video Session 6 Group Discussion Pages 152–160
PERSONAL STUDY DAY 1	Pages 161–166
PERSONAL STUDY DAY 2	Pages 166–170
PERSONAL STUDY DAY 3	Pages 170–174
PERSONAL STUDY DAYS 4 & 5	Complete any unfinished personal study activities

WEEK 6

You're Going to Make It

THIS WEEK'S TRUTH TO HOLD ONTO:

"Someone who's been broken and healed knows how to bring a different kind of peace into each situation they step into because their pain has turned into purpose."

WELCOME AND OPENING REFLECTION:

(Suggested time: 15–20 minutes)

Welcome to session 6 of *Good Boundaries and Goodbyes.*

Leader Note: Have a few people share their response to this question before starting the video:

What was your most helpful takeaway from this week's homework?

VIDEO:

(Running time: 26:00 minutes)

Leader Note: Play the video segment for session 6.

VIDEO NOTES:

Use the outline below to help you follow along with the teaching video and to take additional notes on anything that stands out to you.

Matthew 5:2–12

He said: "Blessed are the poor in spirit,
for theirs is the kingdom of heaven.

Blessed are those who mourn, for they will be comforted.

Blessed are the meek, for they will inherit the earth.

Blessed are those who hunger and thirst for
righteousness, for they will be filled.

Blessed are the merciful, for they will be shown mercy.

Blessed are the pure in heart, for they will see God.

Blessed are the peacemakers, for they
will be called children of God.

Blessed are those who are persecuted because of
righteousness, for theirs is the kingdom of heaven.

"Blessed are you when people insult you, persecute
you and falsely say all kinds of evil against you
because of me. Rejoice and be glad, because great
is your reward in heaven, for in the same way they
persecuted the prophets who were before you.

Hebrews 5:8

Son though he was, he learned obedience from what he suffered.

Mark 14:34a

"My soul is overwhelmed with sorrow to the point of death, . . ."

How in the world could Jesus get to where He was overwhelmed with sorrow to the point of death? In His perfection, He knew everything. If answers would have made it better, he had all the answers.

Jesus knew what it felt like to want the plan changed and to know that God is absolutely capable of doing anything, yet He chose to trust God when He didn't answer His prayer.

I don't think the Beatitudes are just individual groups of people or different seasons of our life that aren't connected. . . . I think Jesus is giving us the stages of brokenness so that we won't get lost when we get so very hurt.

I feel like we are really good with understanding what to do when people grieve a loved one that passes away. . . . But what about the millions of other funerals that we're both having for the disappointments and disillusionments and devastations . . . in life?

There's nothing that can make us more humble or more meek than when we are on our face before God crying out for Him to help us. That brokenness will lead you to a humility that really can be such a beautiful gift.

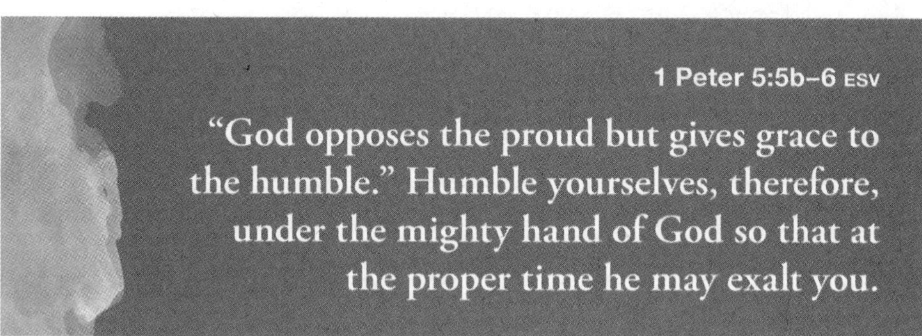

1 Peter 5:5b–6 ESV

"God opposes the proud but gives grace to the humble." Humble yourselves, therefore, under the mighty hand of God so that at the proper time he may exalt you.

Someone who's been broken and healed, they know how to bring a different kind of peace into situations that they step into because their pain has turned into purpose.

Health can't bond with unhealth no more than light can bond with darkness. It only makes sense if you're going to bring healing and light into this world, you will offend the unhealth and the darkness in other people.

There is a purpose in your pain. Embrace it and maybe even thank God for it even though it hurts. Remember, what is so devastating here on earth could be such an epic win in the spiritual realm when we get to heaven.

Group DISCUSSION

(Suggested Time: 40–45 Minutes)

Leader Note: We have suggested questions to start with, but feel free to pick any of the additional questions as well. Consider the timeframe of your group and know the ultimate goal is meaningful discussion.

SUGGESTED QUESTIONS . . .

1. Today's video teaching began with a story about a season with two babies and a pee bag. Now, 27 years later, those babies are grown women and, thankfully, that "bag situation" is no longer! But in that moment, things felt overwhelming. Can you relate to a similar season in your life when it felt like things would stay that way forever?

2. How has today's teaching on the Beatitudes changed or challenged your thinking on this passage of Scripture?

3. Each verse in Matthew 5:3–12 leads us through the various stages of loss and brokenness to a place of healing. Open your Bible to this passage and underline the one verse that seems to indicate the most where you are at right now in your own healing process. Write it below and share it with the group as time allows.

4. So often I want to believe that if I just understood what God was doing, or if I knew what God's ultimate goal was for my suffering, then I would be better able to endure the hardships. But **Jesus knew everything, and He still experienced "sorrow to the point of death."** Are you ever tempted to believe that if you just had the answers, then you would feel at peace about your situation? How does the verse in Mark 14:34 encourage you that having the answers wouldn't be the comfort you desire?

5. Look up 1 Peter 5:5b–6. What is one way you are committed to growing in humility?

ADDITIONAL QUESTIONS . . .

6. When a loved one passes away, there's a whole protocol for us to follow. We know what to wear. We know who to call. We know what to do. We know to bring them a casserole. But we don't know what to do for those other losses in our lives. The heartaches. The disillusionments. The broken dreams. With your group, brainstorm a list of these other losses that don't seem to have a cultural protocol but are still totally devastating in a person's life. Then as a group, generate a list of ideas for how you can personally and collectively come alongside someone who is suffering one of these other losses.

7. If there is purpose to your pain, and I believe there is, do you feel you need to fully understand that purpose in order to embrace what you are going through? How has today's teaching helped you in this area?

8. The final verse in the Beatitudes is, "Rejoice and be glad, because great is your reward in heaven, for in the same way they persecuted the prophets who were before you" (Matthew 5:12). How does this truth anchor you in times of heartache and also give you a vision for hope?

CLOSING: (Suggested time: 5 minutes)

Leader Note: End your session by reading the "Final Personal Studies" instructions to the group and making sure there are no questions pertaining to the homework. Then take a few minutes to pray over your group, either reading the provided prayer aloud over them or praying your own prayer.

FINAL PERSONAL STUDIES . . .

Every week in the *Good Boundaries and Goodbyes Study Guide* includes five days of personal study to help you make meaningful connections between your life and what you're learning each week. This week, you'll work with the material in chapter 12 and the conclusion of the book *Good Boundaries and Goodbyes.*

PRAYER

Father, thank You that You have not left us alone in our sorrows, but You came and dwelt among us in order to take our sorrows upon Yourself. You understand exactly what we are going through, and You extend Your mercy and compassion to us. You live today to intercede on our behalf, and we are so grateful for the love You show us, over and over, time and again. As we move through our brokenness and find healing in Your name, may the beauty in our lives become living testimonies of Your goodness and faithfulness. We love You, Lord. In Jesus' name, amen.

Personal STUDY

Read Chapter 12

Wow. I can't even believe that we're already here, in the final week of this study together. I am so proud of how hard you've worked through these lessons with me, implementing boundaries, communicating consequences, and following through with your words and actions. **You are doing the hard work of trusting in God and applying what He has called us to do in this healing process.** You are building a strong foundation upon which all your relationships can grow healthier and more whole.

Here's a glimpse of what's in store for this week:

In Day 1, we'll talk about moving *through* our grief.

In Day 2, we'll discuss experiencing God *through* every season.

In Day 3, we'll conclude by holding fast *through* God's Word.

If you haven't read chapter 12 yet, please do so before you begin.

1. Please read the book excerpt below and answer the question that follows.

> **"As you move through life, if you are committed to developing humility, growing in spiritual maturity, staying emotionally and physically healthy, and managing your relationships more wisely, you're going to find those gaps ever-widening between where you are and where some of those around you are." (p. 196)**

Those who are for you will celebrate your growth and applaud your healthy decisions, but not everyone will appreciate your efforts. In those cases, the gap between you will widen until you're just not in the same place anymore emotionally or spiritually. When this happens, you will feel the loss, even though you know it's for your health, and theirs, in the long run. So, it's wise to prepare yourself for what you will do when you experience those losses. That's what we'll talk about in today's personal study time. For now, think of some of the losses you've already experienced, or are beginning to experience, as a result of the good boundaries you have begun to put in place. Write down whatever comes to mind.

2. Please read the book excerpt below and answer the questions that follow.

> **"Grief made me face my disappointment. Grief made me realize that my sadness wasn't because I was wanting dead things to come back to life. . . . I had to own the fact that I loved these people for who I thought they would be as a spouse, a family member, a friend, or a coworker, instead of who they actually were. I loved the idea of them loving me well but not how they actually treated me." (pp. 197–198)**

This is so hard. Because this is where I have contributed to the cycle of chaos—with my longings turned into wishful thinking that wasn't based in reality. And when I avoided the grief, I continued to live in this form of denial. But when I accepted that some of those I love are not really who I hoped they would be, then the grief began to wash over me, coming in waves that I couldn't always control. My counselor says **the only healthy way forward is through the grief. I must let grief do its work in me so I can heal and not perpetuate the dysfunction any longer.**

When you experience grief, are you tempted to push it to the side or stuff it back down? Are you tempted to "get over it" quickly so you can move on? Or, are you ready to experience the full force of it, with all its gravity and weight, and begin the grieving process that is really the start of the healing process?

3. In the book I mention that we may experience a million little funerals that no one else attends. They're the deaths and the losses we feel acutely and deeply, but don't always have a name for. They're the hurts that don't always come with protocols. But when we come to a place where we accept the losses and grieve the hurts, we can be released from the

hold they have over us. And one of the ways we can move *through* this grief is by looking to Christ in His pain and suffering. Read Isaiah 53:2–6. How does this prophecy about Jesus describe the reality He lived while on this earth?

4. Knowing that Jesus suffered to such a great extent shows us that He understands our pain, so we can feel safe to bring each and every funeral to Him. Ask Him to stand in the gap between where you are and where you long to be. Read Matthew 11:28–30, and in the space below, write down whatever burdens you are bringing to Him.

5. Please read the book excerpt below and answer the questions that follow.

> **"If I need to cry, I cry. If I need to journal, I journal. If I need to write it all out on paper and tear it up into hundreds of pieces, I do. If I need to then talk it all out with my counselor or a friend, I pick up the phone. But the one thing I don't do is go back to pretending and living in denial. I've accepted this grief. I've had the marked moment of accepting what is and what is not. And it's from this place of acceptance that I will move forward into healing." (p. 203)**

I've listed several of my go-to practices that help me when I am feeling the full weight of my grief. Journaling. Reading my Bible. Writing out my prayers. Talking through my feelings with a trusted friend or counselor. What are some of your go-to practices that you will turn to when you are feeling the full weight of your grief? List them in the space below. You'll undoubtedly want to list some of the ones I've mentioned, but add some more. When you're feeling lost in a sea of loss, these practices can help to anchor us as the waves of our grief hit us over and again.

6. Open your Bible to 2 Corinthians 4:17–18. This is one of my favorite verses because it reminds me that this world—with all its hurts and sorrows—is not all there is. There is a better world waiting for us. And when we can keep our eyes fixed on eternal realities, then we are tethered to truth. Write out these two verses in full. Perhaps even commit them to memory.

7. Finish your personal study time today by reading Psalm 34:18. Write your thoughts below, and thank God that He is always close to the brokenhearted. He saves those who are crushed in spirit.

Read the Conclusion

You are not alone. One of the reasons I am such an advocate for counseling is because a trained counselor can help you name the realities you are facing. When we can put a name on something, we are better able to address it and work through it. And that's part of what I've wanted this book and study guide to do for us—give us strategies that honor God while also helping us move through the heartbreaking realities we're facing.

But most of all, I've wanted you to see that God is with you. He is there when no one else is. He understands when it feels like no one else possibly could. And He gets it. God is for you.

Today we're going to reflect on the conclusion of the book *Good Boundaries and Goodbyes*. If you haven't already read the conclusion, please do so before you begin.

1. Please read the three book quotes below and answer the questions that follow.

> **"[B]oundaries aren't the quick fix that maybe we hoped they would be . . ." (p. 209)**

> **"But the communication, consequences, and consistency that good boundaries provide bring such clarity around what to do when damaging dysfunctions are present." (p. 209)**

> **"[B]oundaries really do serve to help keep us safe and our relationships healthy." (p. 209)**

Good boundaries are good for so many reasons. In the space below, write some additional things you have learned about boundaries and how they are good for healthy relationships.

2. Please read the book excerpt below and answer the questions that follow.

> **"Sometimes what gets me through the hardest parts of my life is knowing I'm not the only one going through it." (p. 211)**

Ideally, you've been working through this study guide and our discussion on good boundaries and goodbyes with a group for the weekly sessions. Why is it so important that we are surrounded with godly friends who can be there for us and when needed give us wise counsel? What does Proverbs 15:22 say about this?

3. Please read the book excerpt below and answer the questions that follow.

> **"The greatest joy in life isn't when it all works out like we hoped it would. It's when we experience the God of the universe pausing to reach us and remind us we aren't alone." (p. 216)**

Let's pause right here and read that again. Now read each of the following verses and then write below the one consistent theme they share: Psalm 23:4; Isaiah 41:10; Matthew 28:20.

4. Read Matthew 1:23. One of the names for Jesus is Immanuel. What does this name mean?

5. So often the world will try to tell us that the main goal in life is to get what we want and be happy, but the Bible tells us a different story. Scripture says that the greatest joy we will ever experience is knowing God. Read 1 Peter 1:3–8. Then write a summary statement that best encapsulates this passage.

6. In the conclusion, I share my story of how God used some words I'd written in my Bible as a teenager to speak to me so clearly of God's love and provision. And my counselor often recommends to his clients that they write a letter to their younger selves. I want to encourage you to do this, too. Write some encouraging words to your younger self. Tell her what you wished you would have known back then and give her your best advice.

7. In the space below write out a prayer, thanking God for being Immanuel, God with us. Thank Him for being with you in every season, both the mountain highs and the valley lows and everything in between.

Today we will continue our personal study time with what we learned in the conclusion as well as the section called "Wisdom to Turn to When Our Boundaries Are Called into Question."

1. Please read the book excerpt below and answer the questions that follow.

> **"It's always been my deep conviction to follow where the Bible leads. I don't ever want to start with my opinions and then find verses to try and support my thoughts. I want to start with God's truth and let Him shape my thoughts with His." (p. 163)**

As much as I pray this book and study guide have been helpful resources for you as you navigate your own relationships, I hope it's also been clear that, first and foremost, we want to be led by the truth of God's Word. Look up each of the following verses and write down what they have to say about God's Word. Spend some time really poring over these truths.

- John 1:1
- Psalm 18:30
- Psalm 119:105
- Isaiah 40:8
- Matthew 7:24
- Matthew 24:35
- Luke 11:28
- 2 Timothy 3:16–17
- Hebrews 4:12
- James 1:22

2. Please read the book excerpt below and answer the questions that follow.

> **"If you ever feel like a verse is being used against you, take time to really dig deep into the meaning. Talk with a trusted friend who studies Scripture, process with a Christian counselor, talk to your pastor, look at commentaries where reliable Bible scholars help unpack verses and their context, and ask the Lord to reveal His intention and heart through the power of the Holy Spirit with these instructions. Finally, look at the principle of the verse and look at the Gospels to see how Jesus handles this principle in the midst of doing life with other people." (p. 230)**

God's Word is our sure anchor. His truth will never fail us. And yet, there are some passages that, when taken out of context, can be used by some to convey a message that was never the intent of the biblical author. When this happens, we're often left confused and hurt. I've listed below some of the verses that are commonly misused, and in the final pages of the book *Good Boundaries and Goodbyes*, I've shared some of the context for these verses to help us understand the principles they actually convey.

Using your Bible and everything you have learned, fill in the spaces below, and if there are any other verses that you can think of that are commonly misinterpreted, I've included some blank rows for you to add your own verses that come to mind.

Verse:	How it's been misinterpreted:	What it actually means:
MATTHEW 5:39		
PHILIPPIANS 2:3–4		

Verse:	How it's been misinterpreted:	What it actually means:
JOHN 15:13		
GALATIANS 6:2, 5		
1 CORINTHIANS 13:5		
1 PETER 3:1–2, 5–6		

3. Read Psalm 107:20 and write it out in the space below.

4. We've unpacked a lot of Scripture today, but before we close, pick one verse from today's study and make it your anthem, the truth that you will write on the tablet of your heart. Then ask God in prayer to help you hold fast to God through His Word even as He holds fast to you.

REVIEW

Use this time to go back and complete any of the reflection questions or activities from previous days this week that you weren't able to finish. Make note of any revelations you've had and reflect on any growth or personal insights you've gained.

Leader's Guide

Thanks for choosing the *Good Boundaries and Goodbyes* video Bible study. Please take a few minutes to read this helpful information before you begin. It should answer most questions you may have.

What Materials Are Needed for a Successful Group?

- Television monitor or screen
- DVD player* (if needed)
- Six-session DVD or streaming video with author Lysa TerKeurst*
- Watch or clock with which to monitor time
- One study guide for each group member (they will be writing in the study guide, so they will each need a copy)
- One copy of the book *Good Boundaries and Goodbyes* for each group member (they will be reading the book between meetings, so they will each need a copy)
- Bible(s)
- Pen or pencil for each person

***Note:** Video streaming access is included with the *Good Boundaries and Goodbyes* study guide. You may also purchase the videos to download or stream online instead of using the DVD.

How Do I Prepare Before the Group Meets?

This video Bible study can work equally well in church and home groups. It is designed to adapt to groups of 90–120 minutes in length. The first thing you need to do is determine how much time your group has available to meet. Then look at the session outline for the group you will be leading. The outline shows suggested times for each section of the study, based on a 90-minute meeting (video times are exact; others are approximate). Depending on your group's specified meeting times, you can decide how you want to allocate your discussion and optional activity engagement.

If you have a group with limited time to meet each week, you can devote two meetings to each session in the study guide. In the second meeting, you can spend the time normally devoted to watching the video to discussing what you got out of the personal study and your reading of the book.

Viewing the video before your group meets will not only help you know what to expect but will help you select the questions in the study guide you want to include.

Make sure the room where you are viewing the video has chairs arranged so that everyone can see the screen. Then when it is time for group discussion, you may need to move chairs so that people in each discussion circle are facing each other. If your whole group will be discussing the material together, having chairs in a semicircle usually allows everyone to see the screen and one another's faces. If your group is large, we recommend that people divide into discussion circles of four to six people; arrange chairs accordingly.

Participants should read the introduction and chapters 1 and 2 of *Good Boundaries and Goodbyes* before the first meeting and video teaching. Prior to each session in the study guide is a schedule of what participants can expect during the coming week. Please be sure to remind group members which chapters to read each week to prepare for the next teaching video. At the end of each personal study time in the study guide these instructions are repeated.

For some people, this study will be exactly what they need to walk them through a hard season or help them process a deep hurt. For others, this might only be the starting place for their healing. Please know there are some difficult realities that only a licensed Christian counselor will be able to help them navigate. At no point in this study should you ever feel the pressure to be someone's counselor. Page 177 lists some resources you can share with anyone in your group who is needing extra help.

Finding a counselor:

American Association of Christian Counselors: www.aacc.net

Focus on the Family: www.focusonthefamily.com

The Proverbs 31 Ministries Podcast: Therapy & Theology Series

Lysa TerKeurst created a podcast series with her personal, licensed professional counselor Jim Cress, as well as Proverbs 31 Ministries director of theology, Dr. Joel Muddamalle, that addresses topics such as boundaries, forgiveness, reconciliation, anxiety, and narcissism. You can find all of these episodes on the official Proverbs 31 Ministries YouTube channel or the Proverbs 31 Ministries website (Proverbs31.org).

GROUP SESSION 1

Boundaries Aren't Just a Good Idea, They're a God Idea

Please have group members read the introduction and chapters 1 and 2 of *Good Boundaries and Goodbyes* before this meeting.

As the leader, personally view the video before your group meets, and review the discussion questions in the study guide to prepare according to your group's time constraints.

Session Outline

Welcome (2–5 minutes)
Opening Reflection (10–15 minutes)
Watch Video (22:00 minutes)
Group Discussion (40–45 minutes)
Closing (5 minutes)

GROUP SESSION 2

A Relationship Can Only Be as Healthy as the People In It

Please have group members read chapters 3 and 4 of *Good Boundaries and Goodbyes* before this meeting.

As the leader, personally view the video before your group meets, and go through the session in the study guide to choose the questions you want to cover.

Session Outline

Welcome and Opening Reflection (10–15 minutes)
Watch Video (28:00 minutes)
Group Discussion (40–45 minutes)
Closing (5 minutes)

GROUP SESSION 3

Maybe We've Been Looking at Walls All Wrong

Please have group members read chapters 5 and 6 of *Good Boundaries and Goodbyes* before this meeting.

As the leader, personally view the video before your group meets, and go through the session in the study guide to choose the questions you want to cover.

Session Outline

Welcome and Opening Reflection (10–15 minutes)
Watch Video (20:30 minutes)
Group Discussion (40–45 minutes)
Closing (5 minutes)

GROUP SESSION 4

Old Patterns, New Practices

Please have group members read chapters 7, 8, and 9 of *Good Boundaries and Goodbyes* before this meeting.

As the leader, personally view the video before your group meets, and go through the session in the study guide to choose the questions you want to cover.

Session Outline

Welcome and Opening Reflection (10–15 minutes)

Watch Video (21:30 minutes)

Group Discussion (40–45 minutes)

Closing (5 minutes)

GROUP SESSION 5

People in the Bible Who Had to Say Hard Goodbyes

Please have group members read chapters 10 and 11 of *Good Boundaries and Goodbyes* before this meeting.

As the leader, personally view the video before your group meets, and go through the session in the study guide to choose the questions you want to cover.

Session Outline

Welcome and Opening Reflection (10–15 minutes)
Watch Video (30:30 minutes)
Group Discussion (40–45 minutes)
Closing (5 minutes)

GROUP SESSION 6

You're Going to Make It

Please have group members read chapter 12 and the conclusion of *Good Boundaries and Goodbyes* before this meeting.

As the leader, personally view the video before your group meets, and go through the session in the study guide to choose the questions you want to cover.

Session Outline

Welcome and Opening Reflection (10–15 minutes)
Watch Video (26:00 minutes)
Group Discussion (40–45 minutes)
Closing (5 minutes)

About the Author

Photograph by Meshali Mitchell

Lysa TerKeurst is president of Proverbs 31 Ministries and the author of more than twenty-five books, including *It's Not Supposed to Be This Way* and the #1 *New York Times* bestsellers *Forgiving What You Can't Forget* and *Uninvited.* But to those who know her best she's just a simple girl with a well-worn Bible who proclaims hope in the midst of good times and heartbreaking realities.

Lysa lives with her family in Charlotte, North Carolina. Connect with her on a daily basis, see what she's working on next, and follow her speaking schedule:

Website: www.LysaTerKeurst.com
(Click on "events" to inquire about having Lysa speak at your event.)

Facebook: www.Facebook.com/OfficialLysa
Instagram: @LysaTerKeurst
Twitter: @LysaTerKeurst

If you enjoyed *Good Boundaries and Goodbyes*, equip yourself with additional resources at:
www.GoodBoundariesAndGoodbyes.com
www.Proverbs31.org

About Proverbs 31 Ministries

Lysa TerKeurst is the president of Proverbs 31 Ministries, located in Charlotte, North Carolina.

If you were inspired by *Good Boundaries and Goodbyes* and desire to deepen your own personal relationship with Jesus Christ, we have just what you're looking for.

Proverbs 31 Ministries exists to be a trusted friend who will take you by the hand and walk by your side, leading you one step closer to the heart of God through:

Free *First 5* Bible study app
Free online daily devotions
Online Bible studies
Podcasts (You might find Lysa's Therapy and Theology series very helpful as you continue your pursuit of staying spiritually and emotionally healthy.)
COMPEL Writers Training
She Speaks Conference
Books and resources

Our desire is to help you to know the Truth and live the Truth. Because when you do, it changes everything.

For more information about Proverbs 31 Ministries, visit www.Proverbs31.org.

An Invitation from Lysa

Photo by Meshali Mitchell

When my family and I were trying to heal from the darkest season of our lives, I kept praying that we'd one day be able to use our experiences to help others find healing. But I didn't just want to do this at conferences. I've dreamed of inviting friends like you over to my home to break bread and share our broken hearts, face-to-face, heart-to-heart. So I'd love to invite you to Haven Place—a safe space for you to find the biblical and emotional healing you've been looking for.

If you'd like more information on the intimate gatherings, Bible studies, and retreats we'll be having here, please visit lysaterkeurst.com/invitation-from-lysa.

I truly believe healing, hope, and forgiveness will be the anthem songs, prayers, and shouts of victory that will rise from this Haven Place.

From the Publisher

GREAT STUDIES

ARE EVEN BETTER WHEN THEY'RE SHARED!

Help others find this study:

- Post a review at your favorite online bookseller.
- Post a picture on a social media account and share why you enjoyed it.
- Send a note to a friend who would also love it—or, better yet, go through it with them!

Thanks for helping others grow their faith!